Praise for the **Students Helping Students** guides:

"These are the kinds of guides a guidance counselor might love, with a mentor's nurturing tone." —*The New York Times*

"As comprehensive and unboring as possible. What sets this how-to apart from others is its tone (think *Seinfeld*) . . ." —*Publishers Weekly*

"Quite different from the usual impenetrable books on the subject written by experts who haven't been in college since 'groovy, man' was, well, groovy . . . This book reminds me of the mantra, 'Each one, teach one.'" —*The Washington Post*

"One of the best qualities of the excellent Students Helping Students® series is the authors' sure sense of college students today [and its] practical, easy-to-absorb bits of advice that can immediately be put into practice . . . [goes] way beyond predictable problems and solutions to offer a full array of possible challenges and useful strategies for solving them." —*Booklist*

"A helpful map to have in your glove compartment–sized dorm room." —*Reading Eagle* (Reading, PA)

"The writing style and tone . . . is wonderful and couldn't be pulled off by someone my age. It's clear that the authors are peer to the reader, which really helps their credibility. I love the slang, the humor, and the way the book is organized. Overall, I love it!" —Julie Jansen, author of *I Don't Know What I Want, but I Know It's Not This: A Step-by-Step Guide to Finding Gratifying Work*

"The fact that it has been prepared by students or recent students has a certain comforting appeal." —*Kliatt*

"A clear and concise guide . . . This informative book is an excellent addition." —*School Library Journal*

STUDENTS HELPING STUDENTS

NAVIGATING YOUR FRESHMAN YEAR

Prentice
Hall Press

A Prentice Hall Press Book
Published by the Penguin Group
Penguin Group (USA) Inc.
375 Hudson Street, New York, New York 10014, USA
Penguin Group (Canada), 10 Alcorn Avenue, Toronto, Ontario M4V 3B2, Canada
(a division of Pearson Penguin Canada Inc.)
Penguin Books Ltd., 80 Strand, London WC2R 0RL, England
Penguin Group Ireland, 25 St. Stephen's Green, Dublin 2, Ireland (a division of Penguin Books Ltd.)
Penguin Group (Australia), 250 Camberwell Road, Camberwell, Victoria 3124, Australia
(a division of Pearson Australia Group Pty. Ltd.)
Penguin Books India Pvt. Ltd., 11 Community Centre, Panchsheel Park, New Delhi—110 017, India
Penguin Group (NZ), Cnr. Airborne and Rosedale Roads, Albany, Auckland 1310, New Zealand
(a division of Pearson New Zealand Ltd.)
Penguin Books (South Africa) (Pty.) Ltd., 24 Sturdee Avenue, Rosebank, Johannesburg 2196,
South Africa

Penguin Books Ltd., Registered Offices: 80 Strand, London WC2R 0RL, England

Copyright © 2005 by Natavi Guides, Inc.
Text design by Tiffany Estreicher
Cover design by Liz Sheehan

PRINTING HISTORY
Prentice Hall Press trade paperback edition/April 2005

Prentice Hall Press is a registered trademark of Penguin Group (USA) Inc.

ISBN: 0-7352-0392-X

Library of Congress Cataloging-in-Publication Information

Navigating your freshman year : how to make the leap to college life and land on your feet /
    Natavi Guides, Inc.
       p. cm.
     ISBN 0-7352-0392-X
     1. College student orientation—United States—Handbooks, manuals, etc. I. Natavi Guides
(Firm)

   LB2343.32.N38 2005
   378.1'98—dc22
                                                                          2004056976

PRINTED IN THE UNITED STATES OF AMERICA

10   9

No doubt you've been bombarded with "expert" advice from your parents, professors, and countless advisors. It's time you got advice you can really use—from fellow students who've been where you're headed.

All Students Helping Students® books are written and edited by top students and recent graduates from colleges and universities across the United States. You'll find no preachy or condescending advice here—just stuff to help you succeed in tackling your academic, social, and professional challenges.

To learn more about Students Helping Students® books, read samples and student-written articles, share your own experiences with other students, suggest a topic or ask questions, visit us at www.StudentsHelpingStudents.com!

We're always looking for fresh minds and new ideas!

A Note from the Founders of Students Helping Students®

Dear Reader,

Welcome to Students Helping Students®!

Before you dive head-first into reading this book, we want to take a moment to share with you where Students Helping Students® came from and where we're headed.

It was only a few years ago that we graduated from college, having made enough mistakes to fill a *War and Peace*–sized novel, learned more and different things than we expected going in, and made some tough decisions—often without having enough advice to help us out. As we thought about our college experiences, we realized that some of the best and most practical advice we ever got came from our class-mates and recent grads. And that's how the idea for Students Helping Students® books was born.

Our vision for Students Helping Students® is simple: allow high school and college students to learn from fellow students who can share brutally honest and practical advice based on their own experi-ences. We've designed our books to be brief and to the point—we've been there and know that students don't have a minute to waste. They are extremely practical, easy to read, and inexpensive, so they don't empty your wallet.

As with all firsts, we're bound to do some things wrong, and if you have reactions or ideas to share with us, we can't wait to hear them. Visit www.StudentsHelpingStudents.com to submit your comments online.

Thanks for giving us a shot!

—Nataly and Avi
Creators of Students Helping Students®

Student Editors

Allison Lombardo is a sophomore at Brown University who now knows more than ever about navigating through the college maze and living on her own. She's learned to call her mother, coerce others into fixing her computer, and hit the snooze button.

Always up for an adventure, she's glad she took the risk to come to Brown. The experiences she had in her first year have altered the life she thought she'd carved out for herself and have opened up opportunities she had never before considered. And that has never been a bad thing. Her future is open, undetermined, and exciting.

Allison would like to thank her parents, her sisters, and her grandmothers for their support. She also acknowledges all of her friends—from home and Brown—who have given her conversation, encouragement, and memories of joy.

Katharine Jackson is a junior at Harvard College. A psychology concentrator in Quincy House, Kate's activities include singing with the Kuumba Singers, dancing with Expressions Dance Company, ushering at Memorial Church, and writing and performing in the Women IN Color Project. She is also a member in organizations such as Women IN Color, the Undergraduate Relations Council, and The Seneca, Inc.

Kate will never forget the difficulties she encountered—academically, socially, and personally—making the transition from her suburban high school in the middle of Ohio to the auspicious gates of Harvard College. She passes on her experiences and insight in the hopes of helping those undergoing the same transition.

Student Contributors

Students from Brown University, Carleton College, Chaminade University, Claremont McKenna College, The College of William and Mary, Columbia University, Dickinson College, Drew University, Emory University, Fairfield University, Fashion Institute of Technology, Harvard University, Middlebury College, Moravian College, New York University, Pennsylvania State University, Quinnipiac University, Richmond University, Rutgers University, Scranton University, Stanford University, Tufts University, Union County College, University of Connecticut, University of Delaware, University of Hartford, University of Pennsylvania, University of Vermont, Vassar College, Wesleyan University, West Chester University, Wooster College, and Yale University contributed their brutally honest advice, ideas, and personal stories to this guide.

Allison's Note

Everyone has some kind of advice for you as you leave for college. Your parents want to relate their experiences, your grandparents would like to tell you what the real world is like, and your teachers want to talk about how wonderful higher education is. But your decision to go to college is not about them or their past—it's about you and your future.

We've put together some tips to guide you through your first year in college and have tried not to bore you with advice you'll be hearing over and over from all the "experts"—your advisors, parents, and professors. Instead, we filled this book with advice from students who've actually survived freshman year and lived to tell about it. Certain things you can only know once you've experienced them.

I was nervous but excited when I was leaving for college, and admittedly, the first few days were a little rough. The whole year was a challenge, composed of ecstatic highs and tearful lows, but it was all worth it. I learned that the only way to challenge myself is to feel uncomfortable and to push myself into strange situations. There is nowhere else I'd rather be.

One of the key lessons I learned was how many options are open to me if only I pursue them. Self-motivation and self-confidence have turned out to be so much more important than I had initially thought. On the more practical side, I learned how to study for more than six hours and how to stay up for three days partying.

Freshman year is the exciting starting point to a life that you now direct pretty much on your own. There's no one right way to do it, just the way that works for you.

—Allison

Katharine's Note

Congratulations on your high school accomplishments and the launch of your college career. Your adventure is just beginning. The next four years will likely be some of the most difficult, challenging, exhilarating, and rewarding years of your life.

The most important piece of advice I can give you (taken from a website relationship advice column years ago) is KFOIT: Keep Fear Out of It. New people, tough professors, a completely unfamiliar social environment, and being away from home can all make your freshman year at college an intimidating experience. But if you spend your college years afraid of failure, of taking risks, trying new things, and taking on tough challenges, you may rob yourself of the most enriching and exciting experiences college has to offer.

So instead, we invite you to open your mind, quell your fears, quiet your insecurities, strengthen your heart, bolster your courage, take a deep breath, and jump off the high dive. You have nothing to lose and a lifetime of wonderful memories and experiences to gain.

—Katharine

Table of Contents

What Freshman Year Really Is

For many of us, freshman year is the first time we'll live away from our childhood homes, our families, and the people we grew up with. Leaving behind all that's familiar and having to adjust to new people and settings, while not letting academics slip by, can be daunting. It *is* daunting. Not only is everything new, but now you have more control over your life and constantly have to make decisions about its direction.

Your first year of college can be filled with dramatic high and low points. One day you meet a new friend with whom you connect better than with anyone from high school, the next day you fail an exam you thought you'd aced. You'll be surprised, you'll be disappointed, you'll be excited, and hopefully, the last thing you'll be is bored.

Freshman year is a unique experience for everyone. Every person, school, state, region, and campus is different. This means party scenes will vary as greatly as academics, rules, and opportunities. There is no typical or right freshman-year experience, and you shouldn't constantly compare yours to what the "right" one might be. Do what makes sense for you because, above all, your first year of college is one of the first times in your life when you get to make your own decisions and stand by them.

Freshman year is the time to keep an open mind and try out new things, from getting involved in activities you never thought of in high school to making friends with people to whom you never thought you'd relate. Testing out new ground sometimes means feeling insecure and uncomfortable, at least for a bit, and one of the best skills the first year of college teaches is how to overcome those feelings. Trust yourself to step out of your comfort zone—there's no better time to do this than now.

What It's Not

Your first year at college is not the most important and will not impact your college education, your career, or your life in a huge way. You have time to try things out and not get them perfect on the first go-around. Everyone in their right mind will forgive a few lower-than-should-be grades on your freshman year transcript. And no one in his or her right mind will care about you dropping out of the Ultimate Frisbee club midway through the year.

This is also not the time to set in stone what you'd like to do in college or with the rest of your life. If you don't take time to explore all of your options, you might settle on one you won't like later. So take the time, and don't pressure yourself to know everything right away. Graduation is four years away, in case you've forgotten.

Freshman year is not a good time to be afraid or closed-minded. Try new things, meet new people, be open to newness in general—it can be so rewarding. Finding out what you don't like is as important as knowing what you love.

Freshman year is definitely not the defining year of the rest of your college experience. If you have an awful one, you can readjust and make the next ones better. If you have an amazing one, you shouldn't stop trying to make the next years as great. Don't get annoyed with all those people calling you a young frosh—as a young frosh you have a license to make mistakes, change, and leave behind whatever you don't think makes your life better.

1

Leaving Home

You know you're an official college student during the moment you wave goodbye to your family from your dorm room. After months of planning out this new life, it's here. But while it's really exciting, leaving home is often harder than most of us expect.

Don't despair, and give yourself some slack as you deal with this change. Even the coolest, toughest football quarterbacks get sad and hesitant about leaving what has been so comfortable and familiar for so long. Even if you're not going far away to college, this is a big transition for you and your family. You're becoming more independent, meeting new people, and encountering new experiences. Most transitions are a challenge.

As you head off to school, here are a few things to keep in mind.

- Take It or Leave It
- It's Time to Say Goodbye

- Remember Old Friends
- Home Strange Home

Take It or Leave It

This may seem obvious, but there are really only a few things that you'll need at college—and many things you'll want to bring. If you lucked out with a huge dorm room—yes, we're all envious—you have much more liberty in deciding what goes with you. For the rest of you, one piece of advice: Don't over-pack. You'll end up being stuck with stuff you won't use, and it will take up precious space that can help keep you sane.

Regardless of your room size, here are some must-haves, in no particular order:

☑ **Computer.** If it's at all possible to buy one or borrow one, do it. Most colleges have pretty good computer facilities that you can use for free, but they're often crowded and noisy, and not in your own room. If you have a choice, opt for a laptop—you can bring it to the library or outside, and can have more options for where to work. But laptops attract thieves, so you might also consider buying a lock to keep your laptop from wandering off.

☑ **Extra socks and underwear.** Doing laundry is expensive and it's a pain. You can always rewear jeans and sweaters, but clean underwear and socks are key.

☑ **Flip-flops.** Using communal showers equals foot fungus, an unattractive yet common problem in dorms. It may feel weird to be wearing shoes to the shower at first, but in the long run your feet will appreciate it.

☑ **Climate-appropriate clothes.** If possible, try to bring only what you'll need for the season and climate you'll be living in. There is usually not a lot of room for extra clothes, especially bulky sweaters or excessive sandals. You can always trade clothes at home during winter or spring break.

☑ **Storage bins.** Stacking things is the way to go in your cell block . . . sorry, dorm room. You can get a huge variety of storage bins in stores like Ikea, Target, or Bed Bath & Beyond.

☑ **Group games.** Board games, cards, and any other communal games will make you popular with your classmates. They are a great way to make new friends and are perfect for fun procrastination.

☑ **Home reminders.** Bring things that remind you of home, such as a few pictures, your old basketball, or posters. It's not childish to show off stuff from home, as long as you don't go overboard, and your new friends will appreciate the stories behind the objects.

☑ **Dictionary and thesaurus.** If you have them, bring them to save money. Although most computer programs have a thesaurus built in, the paper version has many more options.

☑ **Halogen lamp.** Fluorescent lights are cold, kill your eyes, and are not extremely intimate for that late-night date. Get a cheap halogen lamp and you'll use it for years—many recent grads still can't part with theirs. But before you go out and buy one, make sure your college doesn't consider them a fire hazard.

☑ **Clothes hamper.** You want something roomy and something you can easily carry with you when doing laundry.

☑ **First-aid kit.** Just in case. Definitely bring Band-aids.

On the flip side, here are a few things to leave at home, if you can help yourself:

☑ **Twenty favorite books.** You'll be reading a ton of new material, and having dozens of your favorite books nearby can serve as an unwelcome distraction. A few, maybe, but not more than a few.

☑ **A year's supply of cereal and toothpaste.** "Why would I?" you're thinking. Good, keep thinking that. But some have, so we just wanted to make sure—there are stores where you're going and you will be coming home in the next four years.

☑ **100 pictures of your high school sweetheart.** Couldn't just a few do? If you really do love each other, you don't need that many to remember his or her face; and if you don't, then why scare off potential new interests with an in-room shrine?

It's Time to Say Goodbye

Saying goodbye is hard, especially since it's probably the first time you'll be away for such a long time. Your parents are tearful

Allison's Corner

In my mother's and my nervousness over my leaving for school, we overpacked. Buying toiletries in bulk was my mom's way of preparing me for my life on my own. As much as I appreciated not having to buy shampoo all year, it would have saved space and not really affected the money spent if I had just gotten more when mine ran out. Instead, I was left at the end of the year with three untouched shampoo bottles, four extra toothpaste tubes, and a surplus of shaving cream, razors, and toothbrushes.

about their baby growing up and you just don't want to leave your cute puppy behind. Don't worry, you'll be home soon—Thanksgiving is just three months away. (And by then you might not want to leave school at all.)

Be understanding of your parents' feelings and don't be ashamed to feel sad or cry. This *is* a big event for everyone. Reassure them that you'll call and email often—you can decide later just how precisely you'll stick to your promise. Also, although most young siblings will probably pretend that they are happy to see you leave and get your room and stereo, they'll miss you. You don't have to embarrass them by talking about it, but just know that they're sad to see you go.

As you leave, set aside some time to say goodbye so you don't rush it as you run out at the last minute. This isn't cheesy, it's necessary.

Saying goodbye to friends can be extremely weird and emotional. All of you have doubts and fears about the strength of your friendships and have no idea how going away to college might change them. Some friendships fade with time, yet others are successful and remain strong for many years.

Each relationship has a different dynamic so it's difficult to give general advice, but it's a good idea to talk to your friends before you go about how to stay in touch. Exchange email addresses, phone numbers, and assurances that staying in touch is important. If you'd rather not make any commitments, you can always give them a big hug and say: "See you at Thanksgiving!"

The key thing to realize is that saying goodbye is tough for you and the people around you. Take your time.

Remember Old Friends

"You'll make new friends at school, but they cannot replace the relationships you have with those from home. The feeling of the reunion with old friends is priceless."

—Sophomore, Drew University

You know this, of course, but here's a reminder—it takes effort to maintain relationships that matter to you. Call, email, use Instant Messenger, and send pictures. Involve your family and your old friends in your new life and ask them about their own. Good friends are hard to find, and just because you've made new ones doesn't mean that your trusted high school buddies should not be part of your life. Maintaining old friendships can be strenuous, especially as you and your friends are overwhelmed with new experiences at college. Do the best you can, and don't hold too many grudges if your friend doesn't call you for a week—just think of how crazed and busy you are.

Friendships
by Rosaleen, Sophomore, Vassar College

I left a group of about a dozen guys and dolls who had once been inseparable in high school. Over the years certain people became closer than others, but the summer before we went away to school was all about enjoying each other's company and having fun. Now I realize that maybe we were preparing ourselves for a big change in our relationships.

Profundity aside, it was hard to leave home. It's a big step that you make all at once, but, though most people will not maintain all of their friendships, the important ones will remain as consistent and as wonderful as they were when you lived down the street from your friends or saw them every day in the halls.

I've learned that you'll find yourself making an effort to stay in touch with those who were and are most important to you. And while the idea of losing some friends along the way may be scary, it's a part of growing up. The friendships that you'll form in college are on a different level from so many high school friendships, and it's that maturity that takes you from childhood into adulthood. It's scary to think about, but it's great to be a part of.

All I can say is: Don't worry too much. That which will be will be, whether you're scared of it or not.

Home Strange Home

If you're going to college away from home, returning to your stomping grounds for the first time can be difficult. You've got a new life at college and your parents and friends aren't as integral a part of it as they're used to being. You feel strange not knowing all of the details of what went on at home while you were gone and might feel left out.

It might shock you to find out that your family has moved on with their lives, your room is now the den or the computer room—and painted in that gawky green color you can't stand—your siblings are wearing your clothes, and your parents are planning a vacation without you. Weren't they all supposed to just sulk and wait for you to come home? No, and trust us, you wouldn't want that. Your life has changed, and so has theirs,

Apologies
by Brian, Senior, Scranton University

When I came home from college for the first time, things were all the same, except my room always looked different. I guess the whole house did—I noticed the subtle changes around the house much more.

I distinctly remember this being the point in my life where I realized my parents were people who had their own lives. I started realizing that they've made some mistakes just like I have. Living away from home really taught me a new level of respect for my parents. I also found that being away from my sister brought a lot to our relationship. I genuinely felt awful about being such a crummy older brother when we were kids. I think I apologized to her, and if I didn't, I should have.

I also remember actually apologizing to my mom around this time for being such a reckless and brazen teenager. I remember her sitting me down my junior year in high school and asking me to stop drinking so much, then the next day I came home plastered. So, I let her know that I was sorry about being such a "teen."

and you need to adjust to your relationship as independent adults.

Your parents and you might step on each other's toes a bit during your first time back, especially when you come home at four in the morning and they're up waiting for you and asking why you didn't call. Try to be sensitive—yeah, you're on your own now, but they're probably not used to that yet. Just apologize and let them know next time you're planning to be out late. You'll escape to your freedom soon enough when you go back go school.

When you hang out with your old friends, it's fine to describe your new life to them, but be careful to not get competitive about it. Don't compare yourself to them or constantly brag about what a great time you're having. Everyone will feel pressured to be having the ultimate college experience, but in reality it's not easy to be so happy so quickly.

Going to College Close to Home

Going to college close to home might seem like less of an adjustment than going away to school, but it's still a big change. While you know the general area, the campus is a city all on its own and you'll have to adjust to it all the same. You'll be meeting tons of new people and making new friends, and will have to juggle new friendships with old friends who might be going to school at your college or one nearby.

Here are a few hints about dealing with the transition to college if it's close to home:

- Make a special effort to meet new people and forge new friendships. It might be tempting to stick to your old group of friends, but it's important to make new connections as well.

- Talk with your family and set expectations about coming home or them coming to visit you unannounced on a Friday night. Also, if you plan to come home to do laundry all the time, make sure your folks are okay with it.

- Being familiar with the area surrounding your college has some great benefits—offer to show a few of your new friends around, take them to your favorite coffee shop or CD store, or just take a walk.

- If you want to offer a friend to stay over at your family's house for Thanksgiving or winter break, ask your parents first. But this is a really nice gesture that many students who might not be able to fly home for the holidays will really appreciate.

2

Getting Your Bearings

Whether your school has an orientation or not, getting comfortable in a totally new place can be intimidating. Imagine, you've just been dropped off and now you have to fend for yourself. You know no one and have no idea where even the food is. What do you do?

Take your time, don't forget to breathe, and remember that thousands of other people are feeling the same emotions you are. And most importantly, get out there! Locking yourself in your room and hoping that when you come out you'll just magically feel at home definitely doesn't work—too many of us have tried it.

- Which Way to the Library?
- Hi, My Name Is . . .
- A Whole New World
- Don't Be Embarrassed to Feel Homesick

- Play Like a Sponge
- Lap Sit, Anyone?
- Make Friends with Five Key People

Which Way to the Library?

Some campuses are small and easy to navigate; some are large and involve getting around cities. Your new environment may at first seem very intimidating, but if you take a bit of time to explore it, you'll feel more comfortable.

Take a walking tour, if you can, and don't be afraid to use a map. Yes, you may look like a dork, but when you know your way around by the second day, the other freshmen will look at you with awe. Get to know the facilities your school offers, such as the gym, library, eating halls, career center, and fun places to study and hang out. Make the most of your tuition dollars starting with the very first week.

If you're going to college in a different state or town from your own, get to know the culture of the area. All regions have different personalities, and learning about your area's politics and culture will make your four years there more interesting. Take advantage of your surroundings: Urban settings offer a variety of fun things to do, from clubs and bars to art shows and theater, and more rural campuses allow you to enjoy the great outdoors.

Find out how to best get around campus—shuttles, public transportation, and the shortest walking routes. You'll feel more in control if you know how to get where you're going once things get into full swing.

Hi, My Name Is . . .

"In the beginning of the year everyone is in the same boat, knowing no one, so go out of your way and introduce yourself to a variety of people—it will make your year more enjoyable."

—Sophomore, Fairfield University

We might sound like a broken record, but the best way to make friends is to be yourself. You want to find people whom you like to hang out with and who like the real you. If you felt pressured to put up a front in high school, college is the time to be honest with yourself and find a community you enjoy. There's a niche for everyone—find yours and don't be afraid to be open about it.

Making friends is not an overnight process, and introduction after introduction can make you feel overwhelmed. Be friendly, strike up a conversation, and ask questions—people love to talk about themselves. Don't feel sheepish if you need to ask for someone's name again. It's understandable, and you're better off doing it now than three months later. Even if you're generally shy, try to be slightly more social for the first couple weeks so that you don't isolate yourself.

Here are a few fun ideas for meeting people:

- Embarrass yourself—no one will be intimidated by you, and some people may be intrigued.

- Invite a few people to eat an informal lunch or dinner in the cafeteria. It's free, it fosters conversation, and everybody has to eat.

- Introduce people you've met to other people and ask to meet your friends' friends. The more people you meet, the greater your chances of finding the few who will become your closest friends.

- Free food and games draw college students like flies to that sticky paper stuff. No one can resist a homemade cookie or a good party, so give both.

- Keep your room door open when you're in and don't mind being disturbed—you'll be welcoming conversation and your hallmates will be glad to stop by.

- Make an effort to get to know people outside of your dorm by not hanging out there all the time. Stay back after class and talk to your classmates, share a table at the cafeteria, and strike up a conversation near your mailbox.

- Go to open-mike nights, help sessions, and organizational club meetings. You might not enjoy the actual activity, but it's a great way to meet people.

This whole process can be intimidating, but don't worry—everyone is in the same boat and will appreciate your efforts to be nice. Don't put pressure on yourself to form lasting friendships right away; those take time. Just find people with whom you have fun and are comfortable, and the rest will come.

"The first few days of school were orientation and everyone was with his or her family. My family couldn't be there, so I was twice as alone! I started to feel like I had made a mistake about going away from my friends and family to school. But then I saw a girl who was sitting by herself and also didn't seem to have her family there. I went up to her and explained my situation, and I'm not sure who was more grateful to find a friend, she or I. So we stuck to each other like glue for the next few weeks, slowly meeting other people with whom we had interests in common, and then introducing them to one another. By the end of the first month, we had a great group of friends."

—Senior, New York University

A Whole New World

"Being open to new people is the best way to meet lots of them. You may pass by a potential friend if you make too many assumptions."

—Sophomore, Dickinson College

Your university will be filled with students from a variety of cultures, races, and nationalities, as well as social and economic backgrounds. Whether you're from a small Midwestern town, an ethnic neighborhood in the Bronx, or a miniature United Nations in the heart of L.A., expect to meet a lot of people who are different than you. They may have thoughts and ideas that seem radical and might seem even a bit offensive. Be careful not to immediately categorize people by stereotypes based on their race, ethnicity, or where they are from.

If you feel that you're in the minority at your school, try not to be overly sensitive to how other people behave toward you. Without meaning to, the most innocuous look or comment can be perceived as very offensive or snotty. Let your guard down and open yourself up to different people. Those people with whom you never would have been friends in high school may become some of your best friends at college. You never know what you and they might have as common ground.

Try new activities and meet different kinds of people to expand your social sphere. You can always go back to what you're familiar with, but you might surprise yourself as well.

"Don't shy away from making friends with people of different backgrounds and personal interests. Being a football-playing fraternity brother doesn't mean you can't or shouldn't be friends with an a cappella singing member of the Fine Arts Club, nor does it mean that you can't be all those things at once yourself!"

—Junior, University of Pennsylvania

In general, try not to be closed-minded and make judgments based on first impressions. Everyone will have a hard time portraying who he or she really is, and only in time will you see the true person. The same goes for you.

"I'm a fairly mellow guy and I tend not to worry about outward appearances. I sport the finest shoes twenty-five dollars can buy and learned how to tie a tie on my twenty-first birthday. Still, I worried about first impressions weeks before I left for college. What would I wear the first day? Who would I go out with on the first night? What should I first say to a professor I really admire? And so on.

Everyone thinks about 'firsts,' but some obsess over them needlessly. You'll quickly forget the first people you went to the dining hall with on your ninetieth trip there a month later. By then, you'll probably be sitting with new friends and complaining about the food! Likewise, no one will label you by the group of people you go out with on the first night. Don't flatter yourself—no one remembers those kinds of details!"

—Sophomore, Columbia University

Don't Be Embarrassed to Feel Homesick

"I was very lonely for the first few weeks and tried to assuage my loneliness by talking to my high school friends. It's okay to do some of that, but at some point you need to get out and meet people. There's just no way around it. This isn't *Felicity*—your roommate isn't automatically going to be your best friend and your resident advisor your boyfriend. (I actually don't recommend that.)"

—Freshman, Brown University

As much as you couldn't wait to leave and even with all the distractions in your new crazy college life, there will be days when you wish you could shower without shoes and have your mom make you some great pasta. You'll want to hang out with the friends who really know you and like the same TV shows you do, and maybe you'll even dream about fighting with your brother or sister or walking your dog.

Never fear—feeling homesick is common when you first enter a new situation and everything you've ever known is far away. Honestly, it's not as bad as it sounds, but it does happen to everyone at some point. It's okay to feel down or be moody, but don't mope around for too long. Try to distract yourself by exploring your new home and making new friends. Bug your roommate, hang out with your hallmates, go for a run around campus, or read through the course catalogue and circle classes you'd really like to take. Do something, anything, to remind yourself of why you like where you are.

Also, don't pressure yourself to feel comfortable right away. Making good friends takes time, but by Thanksgiving you'll have plenty of new memories. In fact, you'll probably feel like school is your home.

It's also okay to give in to feeling homesick once in a while. Call your parents, email your friends, hang up some pictures of last summer's fun, send postcards to your siblings, or even listen to some music that reminds you of home. Being a freshman means that there is a long period of adjustment because living away is a new thing for you and you're forging your own community. Give it time and ask mom to send some cookies.

 Allison's Corner

As excited as I was to get out of my house and be on my own, after a few days I missed my own room and house and the living animals in it. I missed my two sisters like crazy because no one at school wanted to wrestle and make fun of each other like we do. I also missed my parents, and not just their home cooking but also their company. It got easier as months went on and I made new friends, but I don't think that I can totally stop feeling homesick from time to time.

Cold
by Diana, Senior, Tufts University

I crossed the Mason-Dixon line on my way to move into Tufts and breathed a sigh of relief that toppled trees in a five-mile radius. At last I'd escaped my narrow-minded high school, rigid parents, and hometown in Georgia that was eerily reminiscent of *Deliverance*. On Thanksgiving, my parents could visit *me* because I was never coming home.

But the first thing I missed were the words, "How are you to-day?" Then I started to notice the silence, how conversations ceased the second people stepped into an elevator and how everyone was so rushed they merely bucked their head or threw up a hand as they raced by without ever stopping to chat. I made dear friends on campus, but in general, Northeasterners seemed so cold and distant. I was accustomed to treating strangers as feeling human beings worthy of your attention and respect rather than robots that should give you what you want, when you want it, and to shut up in the meantime.

And other things were cold besides the people. I missed swimming in October, hot home-cooked meals, and the room I didn't have to share with a roommate who ran the AC full blast 365 days a year. When I tried to confess my homesickness, my new friends couldn't help but snicker at my southern drawl and inevitably commented on how it would only get colder until March. They couldn't understand that the weather wasn't the real issue because they never fully left home. Most students at Tufts grew up in the Northeast and could catch a train to Jersey whenever they needed mom to do their laundry.

I suffered through a pretty bleak winter and felt like I was a failure for missing home. Only a redneck could miss Macon, Georgia, I thought. I had a good year all in all, but I still raced home after my last exam that spring. I had to spend a month or two back home to recognize all the things I love about the South *and* all the things I missed about Tufts. I missed my friends and all the thoughtful students with diverse backgrounds from whom I had learned all year. I also missed the intellectual climate and often found Macon more boring than ever. And yet, I felt at home.

Homesickness is okay. In fact, my time away revealed the two aspects of my personality, and I arrived at a deeper understanding of myself, my values, and my country. Since I couldn't have mom do my wash and dad handle my taxes, I became more independent and resourceful. My relationship with my parents took a 180-degree turn for the better. I now appreciate difference and therefore think about people, society, and a restaurant menu in a whole new way.

Play Like a Sponge

The first few days of school are crazy, and you're sure to be overwhelmed with everything new that's coming at you: new classes, new people, new professors, new routines, and expectations. Try not to get ridiculously stressed during the first few weeks; you'll figure everything out eventually.

Stay on top of things and be organized as you're showered with dozens of pieces of paper and information. It's impossible to figure out how everything works at once, but reading over the informational material you get can be helpful. Don't feel like you have to figure out everything by yourself, either. Bond with your roommate or someone you met and liked as you both step through the initial maze together.

Don't be afraid to ask questions for fear of embarrassment.

Allison's Corner

I can only deal with an overload of information a little at a time, so my solution to the overwhelming paper influx was to dump it all in a drawer. My "Drawer of Fun" has only been investigated when I need specific information. I may not be the best-informed person on campus, but at least I know where my resources are when I need them.

As trite as this sounds, it's very likely that other people have the same question but are too scared to ask. It's important to assert yourself and figure out what you need to know. You may have to be a little dorky to get the information you need, but in the long run you'll be hot stuff for knowing how to work the system while everyone else is still lost.

Lap Sit, Anyone?

"You might feel left out at first, probably scared and nervous, but hang in there. It may take you a few weeks, even a few months, but you'll find your niche. Your place to fit in is out there somewhere and you'll find it sooner or later."

—Junior, Cornell University

Sure, there are probably a few orientation events that turn you off as soon as you read about them. Perhaps you're not a fan of circular lap-sitting or can't stand the wilderness. But try to go to as many orientation events as you can, even if you don't love the actual activity. It's good to get out and meet people—and not just incoming frosh but upperclassmen and even professors, who often organize these activities.

If your school has a special orientation program off campus, such as camping or volunteering to build houses, go if you can. These can be amazing for really bonding and getting to know people in your class. Being off campus is just more liberating somehow, and facing challenges together is a great experience.

Make Friends with Five Key People

"Try not to confuse independence with isolation. Successfully independent individuals make choices based on information gained from consulting with others in their community. There are so many faculty and staff in the college whose job it is to help freshmen make the most of college—don't neglect them."

—Dean of Freshmen, University of Rochester

Everybody's college experience may be unique, but here's one thing that's guaranteed: At least once in your college career, something will go horribly, terribly wrong. Black smoke spews from your heater, your laptop disappears—you do keep it locked, right?—or the registrar inadvertently signs you up for a graduate seminar. Now is the time when you want to have some friends in high places who can deal with your problems while you worry about papers, problem sets, and parties.

In particular, get to know the following people, then tap them as resources when you need them:

1. **Your resident advisor (RA).** During orientation, you'll meet your RA, tour the campus with your RA, and eat dinner with your RA. Then you make other friends and lose touch with your RA. This a reminder that your RA is living in that large single for free, so don't hesitate to call when the toilet's clogged, your obnoxious neighbors are blasting techno music at three in the morning, or even when you just want to talk with somebody about your midterm.

2. **Your deans/advisors.** Unless you go to the Paragon of Efficiency University, the infrastructure of college is a mishmash of bureaucracy. Talk to your deans about your college goals and they'll help you make a four-year plan, tell you who in the college can help you meet your goals, and help you deal with any red tape involved.

3. **Secretaries.** Secretaries know everybody. If you've got a problem, a secretary can tell you who has the answer.

4. **Your building super (if you don't live in a dorm).** Things break. Fuses blow. Light bulbs burn out. Keys stop unlocking doors. Frisbees fly through windows. It's a good idea to know somebody who can fix things.

5. **Reference librarian.** Research papers are hard enough without wasting time rummaging through the library. Have a reference librarian do your rummaging for you. It'll give you more time to actually write your paper. Besides, reference librarians seem to enjoy it.

3

Avoiding Living Hell

Being randomly paired with a person whose only similarity to you is their gender and being required to spend a peaceful year in a ten-by-ten room is a relatively unreasonable expectation. Even living with your best friend would result in a conflict occasionally. So brace yourself for the worst but be openhearted for the best.

Keep in mind that your freshman-year roommate does not have to be your best friend. You don't even have to pretend to like each other, but you should try not to make yourselves miserable. Approach this new person with an open mind and remember that everyone has a different background and weird habits, even you. Be considerate and willing to compromise, but don't be passive. Your room is your space, too, so assert yourself and form a respectful relationship with your roommate as you remember kindergarten and learn how to share.

- No Time for Lies
- First Impressions Don't Always Count
- I Have to Live Here?!
- Take a Chance on Me
- Rules of Engagement
- Learn to Share
- You've Been Sexiled!
- Escape Pod
- Housing Options Galore
- It's Time for a Change

No Time for Lies

You might be tempted, but don't lie on your roommate questionnaire to make yourself look good. No one cares about how early you like to get up and study. The only thing the questionnaire will be used for is to pair you off with someone moderately similar to you, so be honest.

If you smoke, don't deny it or minimize the actual degree to which you do it; a roommate who doesn't will nag you endlessly. If you're pretty quiet and don't like rock 'n roll blasting till one in the morning, say so—you're not being uncool, you're making sure that your ears survive the year. Even if you vow to yourself that you're going to go to bed early once you get to college, be honest and admit it if you're a night owl.

You get the point: Be honest and don't make stuff up. After you're done filling it out, read your questionnaire and see if it sounds like it describes you. It should at least get your daily habits right.

First Impressions Don't Always Count

When your room assignment letter arrives in the summer, you'll stare blankly at the name and home address, wondering who this stranger is and what lies in store for both of you. So, the first step is to call your roomie and try to make some kind of human contact. You can call under the pretense of planning what you'll each bring to the room, but use this small talk to get to know something about each other.

Just remember not to get too attached to your first impression. Talking on the phone to someone you don't know is not natural, and it's hard to really be yourself for both of you. Take it easy.

On this somewhat uncomfortable phone call, you should discuss practical things, such as whether you're going to have a fridge and, if so, who's bringing it. Try to think of any big items that you'll definitely need in your room, but keep in mind which are essential (a phone) and which are not (a couch). Are you willing to share stereos? Should one of you buy a microwave? Remember: Money is important and you'll want to split things pretty evenly. Also, keep in mind that whoever buys an item will most likely get to keep it next year when you change rooms.

Our advice is to avoid buying things to share and splitting their cost. This can cause some tension at the end of the year when you have to decide who keeps the item and how much the other person should pay for it. Stick to bringing things to share—you bring the stereo, your roommate brings the fridge.

I Have to Live Here?!

Most college rooms are small, have cinder block walls, and look like jail cells—not exactly what you saw in the brochure, right? You might be one of those people who could care less about the way your room looks. If you're not, then use your creativity to spruce it up and make it more like something you can call your home.

- Use halogen lamps instead of overhead fluorescent lighting.
- Buy a few plants and put them somewhere where they can get light.
- Cover at least some of the cold linoleum floor with a colorful rug.
- Put up posters and pictures that you like, remembering to leave some wall space for your roommate.
- Organize your stuff in stackable bins or milk crates so that it's not thrown all over the room.

 Allison's Corner

The first day of school my roommate and I bought this tiny, beautiful plant and named it Mikali. As the year wore on, our baby grew at a rapid rate and began to look like it was from the Little Shop of Horrors. When it started spewing seeds over our windowsill, we had to change Mikali's name to Oscar because the plant simply grew too evil. Our laughter and fear over Oscar brought us together, and at the end of the year we battled over the custody of our surprising, terrifying treasure.

We Talk With . . .

Deepy, Senior, Brown University

How do you make your dorm room the "hot spot"?
First and foremost, make sure you have Lil' Kim's "Hotspot" blaring through your speakers.

No. For real.
The most inviting room I ever saw said "Free Cookies Inside." If you need friends, offer food.

So besides food, what else creates a welcoming atmosphere?
A comfy chair. Board games. Pop—oh wait, I'm from the Midwest; I mean soda.

What makes a room hip?
Old-school Nintendo helps out a little. Sure, your GPA might drop a few points, but having video game buddies is worth it. Oh, and a fridge, too!

What makes a bad room?
Crusty food on the floor. Stuffed animals if you're a guy. Underwear hanging all over to dry if you're a girl. Door closed. Too many pictures of yourself. Too many pictures of your friends and your so-cool home social life.

What about wall coverings?
Avoid the mass, cliché posters. Go for something unique. Like a giant picture of your mom—just kidding.

Put a little creative effort into making your room look and feel like a comfortable place. It will pay off that one horrible day when you flunk a pop quiz, spill soda on your new jeans, and run to your room for escape. Escapes should feel good.

Take a Chance on Me

Whatever your roommate situation might be, here are a few initial rules of engagement to keep in mind:

- **Be friendly.** Whether you're usually outgoing or keep to yourself, make an effort initially to talk to your roommate, to relate, and to just hang out together. You don't have to try to be friends, but making an effort to be nice will pay off.

- **Give each other space.** This is tough if you're literally sharing one room rather than a small apartment where each of you can have some privacy. If your roommate comes back from a shower, maybe you can step out for a few minutes so that he or she can change. Or if you need to make a private phone call, ask if your roommate won't mind giving you a few minutes. These are small gestures, but the effort counts, and your roommate might follow suit.

- **Don't try to do everything together.** If you click with your roommate, then by all means, hang out, go to orientation, and sit together in the dining hall. But don't force it—you'll have a long time to get used to and to get to know each other. Too much time together initially can potentially backfire.

In general, recognize that you don't need to be best friends, or even friends, with your roommate. If you are, great, but if not, all you need is someone you can get along with.

Rules of Engagement

"Once things start to go badly, try to grin and bear it. That works until your roommate breaks out his turntables and plays the most mind-stabbingly bad 'music' you've ever heard. That's when you pretend to be asleep. Once your roommate does things that are not silenced by sleep (smoking, eating smelly foods, singing, etc.), you must politely request a few rules."

—Sophomore, University of Hartford

For those of you without siblings, your roommate will be the first person with whom you'll truly have to share. This might seem like an elementary skill, but it's hard to totally immerse yourself in the culture of dual use if you've never shared a small room before. The most important thing to do in the first weeks of school is to make general rules with your roommate about how you want your room to be so that you can both be happy. If you and your roommate are compatible, this will be easy; if not, this will be necessary for your mutual sanity.

The most basic rules deal with hours. There's a time for music and dancing and a time for the sound of silence. Try to work out some simple rules, such as Monday through Thursday after 9:00, your room will be for studying only. Or, if you both like to party, agree to blast your music well into the night. If you like to study in your room, assert yourself and make sure your roommate knows that you need quiet time. At the same time, remember that you can also study in the library, so be reasonable.

Visitors can also be an issue. If your roommate's friends like to gab at two in the morning while you're sleeping, you should politely ask them to be quiet and should talk to your roommate about having people over late at night. Along the same lines, bedtime is an essential discussion. Hopefully you'll both have honestly filled out your rooming questionnaire and can agree on what time the lights go out. Even if you don't go to bed at the same time, one of you can always use your desk lamp or even go to the library.

The most important thing is to be respectful and compromise—this is a home for both of you. You have the right to be comfortable in your own room but need to give that same freedom to your roomie.

"Show as much respect as you can to your roomie, and always consider how he or she might view the things that you do. Just be assertive and talk openly about things that bug you. Even if you try to show that something bothers you, your roommate may have absolutely no idea."

—Sophomore, Rutgers University

Learn to Share

Everyone has a lot of stuff and there is very little space—try to split things fairly. For instance, if your roommate gets the larger closet, you should get the larger dresser. Also, try to use the space under your bed efficiently. Lofting beds when possible can save a ton of space and leave room for a couch or a beanbag.

When putting up decorations, don't monopolize all of the wall

We Talk With . . .

Ellen, Freshman, Brown University

Did you have a horror roommate experience during your freshman year?

My freshman roommate left the window open all the time, even when it was twenty degrees out, and went to bed at 10:30 every night. When she got sick after midterms, she blamed my typing and having a light on while she was trying to sleep for making her sick. Needless to say, we fought constantly. I ended up doing most of my work in a friend's room.

What was your biggest social challenge in getting adjusted to college?

Socially, college was a little daunting. I graduated from a small school—there were ninety kids in my graduating class. After seeing the same people over and over for eight years, it was amazing, but a little scary, to be in a place where it seemed like I never saw the same person twice.

What was the hard part about making friends on campus?

Getting those friends to do things. At the beginning everybody feels really swamped with work and meetings, and just doing laundry seems like an insurmountable task. When things settle down, it's easier to catch up with new friends.

space, unless your roommate doesn't mind. You can survive without every single one of your favorite posters on the walls, really. And don't make disgusted faces when your roommate puts up a decoration you hate—it's definitely something you can deal with.

A Few Words on Phone Etiquette

"The only phone jack in our room was near my roommate's bed. It was awful because I always felt like I was borrowing her phone, even though it was for both of us. I ended up making a lot of calls from the pay phone in the campus center."

—Recent Grad, Wesleyan University

The phone has the dubious distinction of being at the core of many disagreements and fights between roommates, especially if you only have one line in your room. Who uses it, when, how often, and with how much privacy are all issues that will invariably come up.

If you know that your roommate religiously calls his girlfriend every night at 8:00, be nice and don't hang on the phone during that time. And if you need privacy to talk to someone, just ask. No need to make it a huge deal, but you should recognize that unless you're both considerate, there will be conflicts.

Another way to avoid phone quarrels is to have a cell phone. You can get one pretty inexpensively—a basic plan, usually with free long distance, can run you from $40 to $60 a month—and maybe save yourself a lot of trouble.

Cleanliness is important to everyone, although to different degrees. Now that you share a space with someone, you'll have to pay a bit more attention to keeping that space somewhat clean. Odor is not a good thing. So if your shoes smell, be polite and leave them outside. If you're sloppy, try to contain your mess to your side of the room and not infringe on your roommate's territory.

Privacy is a hot commodity at college, and both you and your roommate will need some. Be respectful and give privacy, and be assertive and ask for it. Some private time will come naturally as you both go about your days and different schedules. But sometimes it will take effort and one of you will have to leave the room for a bit.

Eventually you'll probably learn to read each other's cues, but at the beginning, don't be afraid to speak up.

You've Been Sexiled!

We might have made it up, or you might have heard it before, but sexile is definitely at home in the college student's vernacular. Combine "sex" and "exile" and you get the following situation:

You've just arrived home from a party, and your door seems to be locked. "No problem," you think, as you swiftly whip out your key. Falling through the door, you stumble and see a blur of sheets and flesh. As you rush out covering your eyes in shame, your roommate emerges, fixing her shirt, and apologizes profusely, but asks if she can have the room to herself tonight. You, our friend, have been sexiled.

The best way to deal with these situations, whether you're the lucky sexiler or the sexilee, is to plan ahead. Add these kinds of situations to your "things to discuss on the first day" agenda.

When possible, prenotification is the best option. If you know you'll be having a "guest," ask your roommate if he or she could bunk with someone else for the night. If it's an impromptu sleepover, you should agree on an inconspicuous sign to alert the other not to enter. Whether it's a sticky note or a smiley face drawn on the board hanging on your door, this will indicate to enter only with caution—and if possible, not to enter at all. If you absolutely need to get into the room even with the sign on, knock loudly and wait. When you go in, grab only what you need and look down as you leave.

> "I came home and was promptly asked to leave, but seeing that it was raining, I had nowhere to go and was stuck inside my apartment. Sitting in the hallway that had recently been coated with polyurethane, I inhaled the fumes all night and made some ridiculous phone calls. Grrrrrrr."
>
> —Sophomore, Fashion Institute of Technology

The most important thing about using your room for sexual endeavors is to respect the other person. Leave their side of the room out of it and be clean. The ultimately important thing is to never, ever make out with someone when your roommate is in the room. That's rude and disrespectful to all parties involved. It's hard to forgive a traumatic thing like that. Don't do it.

Escape Pod

> "The best and worst thing about dorm life is that there is always something to do and someone to do it with. It's great to say that you're never bored, but hard not to get distracted."
>
> —Sophomore, Richmond University

A great benefit of living in a dorm is that there are many people other than your roommate with whom you can spend time without going far. No better way to diffuse roommate tension than to get out of the room for a bit and cool off. Get to know your dormmates, spend time hanging out with them, and leave your door open when you feel like having visitors.

> "I'd never lived in a dorm before and it was pretty overwhelming to have people barge in and out of our room during orientation. But after the initial shock, the dorm proved to be a great social setting. Don't worry too much about privacy, especially during the first few months of intense friendmaking."
>
> —Recent Grad, Wesleyan University

Take advantage of the social vibe dorm life has to offer. If you need a quiet place to study, the library is usually your best bet. Leave your dorm room for relaxing and socializing. Investigate common areas in the dorm and find out what amenities your dorm might have to offer in the way of kitchens, game rooms, fitness centers, and practice rooms. These are wonderful resources to have at your disposal, as well as great places to meet like-minded dormmates.

Just make sure that you do get "outside" from time to time and make contact with people not from your dorm. It's healthy and it helps to avoid isolating yourself with a certain group of people.

A common dorm problem is hall noise. What do you do if your neighbors are blasting music at four in the morning when you're trying to sleep? Calmly ask them to turn it down. Don't yell, don't appear overly angry or annoyed, just ask. And make sure to have some earplugs nearby in case the lowered volume still doesn't cut it.

Comic Relief: *Laundry Days*
by Jay, Junior, Columbia University

Sooner or later, it happens: You run out of socks, underwear, or clothes in general, and you're reduced to walking around campus naked. Don't let nudity happen to you!

I stared into the face of nudity several times freshman year, and I was only able to pull through each near-naked experience by dragging three bags of dirty clothes down to the laundry room—six washers and six dryers for six hundred students. Every trip down to the laundry room is fraught with suds and lint, and I always make sure to say a little prayer to the Laundry Gods: "Please, don't shrink my clothes or let the colors run," before my ritual sacrifice of detergent and fabric softener. The Laundry Gods, however, have a sense of humor.

In my first near-naked experience, I got into a fight with a dryer (but the dryer started it). The dryer claimed that it was "done," but my clothes weren't dry. So I used my male fix-it intuition and kicked the dryer. Oddly enough, my clothes were still wet. I hadn't kicked the dryer hard enough, but after several more rounds with the dryer, I gave up and took my wet clothes back to my room in defeat. I hung underwear on my floor lamp and socks from my TV antennas, and the next morning, I avoided nudity but not dampness. The lesson: If the dryer doesn't work, you must kick it harder than I can.

There was another near-naked experience where the Laundry Gods decided to mix in with my clothes some underwear that was, um, more feminine than my typical underwear.

The lesson: If you find women's underwear in your laundry, and you don't wear women's underwear, don't tell your floormates because they will laugh at you and make the same unfunny joke that you are thinking of right now.

"Don't be uptight about keeping things clean in your room or keeping the noise down. Getting mad at people is just frustrating and more annoying to you than to them."

—Junior, Moravian College

Housing Options Galore

While more often than not you'll end up in a double during your freshman year, other possible arrangements include having a single or sharing a few rooms with three or four people. Each has positives and negatives, so do your best to make the best out of your situation.

Having a single means you have the privacy to do whatever and whenever you want. As wonderful as this sounds, singles can often be lonely places, and you have to make a concerted effort not to isolate yourself. Especially in the first few weeks, keep your door open and make friends with the people in your hall. Since you have no roommate, take advantage of your space and invite people over—leave your door open when you're at home and don't mind some company.

Having multiple roommates sometimes presents a greater challenge than living with just one person. All of the issues that we've just talked about apply here, and in greater magnitude, so talking stuff out and setting a few rules is important. Having a room meeting is a good idea once in a while.

Living with more people can give you a great group of friends and allow you not to spend a concentrated amount of time with just one person. But living in a group can create its own issues. Never, ever talk behind one roommate's back to the other roommates—it's not fair to isolate anyone and it can seriously backfire. Also, don't obsess if your roommates seem to bond better than you with them. This happens. Find friends outside of your room and spend time with them.

It's Time for a Change

It happens: You've tried, talked, made rules and broken rules, and it doesn't work. You're stressed out, your grades are slipping, and you stay out as late as you can to get back to your room when your roommate is already asleep. You hate your living situation and, yes, you might be at a point when you need to think about changing rooms.

This is a difficult and last-resort option, so don't take it lightly. If you're the one moving out, you'll have to readjust to a new roommate—unless it's a single—and new hallmates, and will have to go through the initial steps all over again. (Plus, it's a pain to pack up all of your stuff and drag it across campus.)

Having said that, if you really do need to change your living situation, do it. It's definitely possible and freshmen do it all the time. Talk to the people in your residential life office, explain the situation to them, and politely request a new room. In some cases, you'll be asked to wait until next semester to move.

Confronting your roommate about your move isn't easy, even if you don't get along. He or she might be relieved to get rid of you but will likely be a bit hurt and annoyed to have to deal with a new roommate and adjustments that come with the change. Don't be overly mean, just say that you're moving out and that you think it will be better for both of you.

4

Getting to Work

Yes, indeed. Studying and learning is your work for the next four years. And compared to the many mundane jobs out there, this isn't so bad. You'll read interesting books, learn about things you've never learned about before, be inspired by an amazing professor—or a few, if you're lucky—and maybe, most important, you'll get a bit closer to knowing what it is that interests you in life and what you'd like to do with it.

Sometimes college academics can feel overwhelming, and most of us have spent many a night wondering how we're going to get it all done. But with some organization, persistence, and tons of caffeine, you can get it done and even find a few hours to get some sleep.

- Don't Be Hit by a Truck
- Exploration Time
- Schedule Carefully

Don't Be Hit by a Truck

As too many people have probably told you already, college is nothing like high school, not socially and definitely not academically. Although some high schools are more geared toward teaching collegiate skills, almost nothing can prepare you for the shock you feel when you read your first class syllabus or paper assignment.

Don't panic. Take a deep breath and remember that you wouldn't be here unless you could handle it. The admissions committee didn't make a mistake or do you a favor. You were admitted because you're smart and can succeed in your academics. You're just going to have to work for it.

Here are a few suggestions to help you stay on top of things:

- **Prestudy.** While you get into the swing of things, you'll make your life easier if you read some of the material for your classes before each class. No one says that you have to maintain this practice for the next four years, but it's a good way to ease into college academics. When you come to class familiar with the material, you'll be able to grasp much more and do better on exams and papers.

- **Take notes.** As you read class material and listen to lectures and discussions, write down the key points. These will be your own personal Cliffs Notes as you review the material later to prepare for exams or write papers. Don't write down verbatim what the professor is saying. You can't write and listen well at the same time and will risk missing important points. Instead, write down in your own words what you think the most important points are, both from your professors and your reading. Putting things into your own words helps you remember them better.

- **Participate.** Volunteer to answer questions in class. Ask questions. Go to study sessions and help sessions. Get to know your teaching assistants (TAs) and professors and make an effort to talk to them outside of class. By getting involved with each class, you'll feel more like a part of its community of students. You'll also get the most from each class and learn important hints about how to do well on exams and papers.

Exploration Time

"Remember to pursue a broad education, in addition to preparing for a career or graduate program. Just consider the successful people you admire, and chances are, with rare exception, their education was more important than their credentials."

—Vice Provost for Undergraduate Education,
Dean of the Freshman-Sophomore College, Stanford University

Allison's Corner

I did relatively well in high school and felt much like a superstar senior as I arrived on campus. Quickly, I learned that everyone else was also a superstar senior and they were extremely intelligent and talented. I was, and sometimes still am, intimidated by the skills of my peers. Instead of putting myself down about it, I've realized how much I can learn from these smarties and hope that somehow my skills can contribute to the learning community as well. Having confidence about your own skills can be difficult. But remember, you're here to learn from other students as well as from books and professors, and you bring a lot to the mix.

You might be the most focused person in the world and have known from age five what you want to do with your life. Or you might be someone who is interested in many things and disciplines. Or perhaps you haven't yet found that one subject or activity that makes you impassioned. Regardless, freshman year should be your time to explore and really step out of your comfort zone. Don't worry about your career or even your major at this point. You have plenty of time to decide on each.

Instead, try to take a wide variety of classes, including some in which you never thought you'd be interested. How do you know that you don't like art history if you've never taken an art history class before? However diverse your high school's course selection might have been, it probably wasn't as great as your college options. Take advantage of them and explore. A math buff all your life? Try a sociology class. Always wanted to be a doctor? Consider an econ or political science class. Give your mind some new

We Talk With . . .

Frank, Junior, University of Connecticut

What was your first semester like academically?
Horrible. I can't even tell you my GPA.

Why so bad?
Slacking off. Not doing any work. Not caring.

What made college so different from high school?
In high school, you didn't have to prepare for class the next day. You could just show up and if they went over something you didn't know you could ignore it or make an excuse about where your homework was. If you showed up, basically, they would pass you. I thought it would be the same at a state school. Unfortunately, in college you have to show up every day and perform.

What could you have done differently to avert disaster?
I should have gotten to know people who could have helped me, like professors or deans. I should have participated in class.

Any advice?
College is kind of like ice cream. It enriches, but it can be cold. Choose your flavor well, err on the side of caution, and think about how you'll be the next day. Respect it.

food to chew on and you never know, you might surprise yourself.

"Read the *entire* course book. Look into subjects in which you wouldn't naturally be interested to find random cool courses. You might discover along the way that you really don't like physics but instead want to produce records with the skills you acquired in your hip-hop class. Keep your mind and options open for the future."

—Junior, Harvard University

You'll probably have a few requirements to fulfill during your freshman year, and in some cases, your first semester's curriculum will be predetermined for you. Don't necessarily view requirements as evil—they're a great tool to force you to take a variety of classes in different disciplines.

As you choose your classes, try to have a good mix of large lectures and smaller discussions. These tend to be very different, and you should try out both.

Don't always go for what seems to be the easiest class. Go for what seems the most interesting or one that has a great prof.

Schedule Carefully

Having an early class will not "keep you honest" about getting up in the morning if you're not a morning person. What it might do is help you to miss class a lot, as you give into hitting the snooze button ten times. Be realistic.

If you're a morning person, schedule early classes and get them out of the way to have the rest of your day free to study and play. If you can't make a coherent sentence before ten or eleven, keep that in mind and perhaps choose a few afternoon classes.

It's also a good idea to have a few lighter days in your schedule. Having a chunk of free time a few days a week will give you a chance to unwind, get a ton of work done on a paper for one of

Allison's Corner

I like to stay up until 4:00 am and get up around 10:30 am. For some reason I thought that scheduling a 9:00 am class on Monday, Wednesday, and Friday would get me up and out of bed. I liked that class a lot and sacrificed my Thursday nights out and my early morning jogs for it.

However, most days I would fall asleep in class or have to come back home to nap all afternoon. Second semester I scheduled all of my classes for 11:00 am or after so this way I would be up and ready for class and could also enjoy my nighttime studying by candlelight.

your classes, or devote your energy to a favorite extracurricular activity.

Don't try to impress your friends by taking more credits your freshman year than your school generally suggests. You don't want to get burned out, and you need to leave yourself some room to do things outside of class, whether it's getting to know your new friends, playing a sport, or spending time on extracurriculars. Besides, if you take on too many credits, you'll go crazy trying to study for each class and get good grades—and you have enough things to make you go crazy your freshman year.

"When choosing classes, think also about the kind of work each requires. I try to balance reading-intensive classes like history with some that require short spurts of work, like math."

—Junior, University of Pennsylvania

Catching Up

by Jamay, Sophomore, Brown University

I think the toughest part about making the transition from high school to college is getting used to the idea that your work will never "be done." In high school, work was mostly short-term. If you finished your weekend's homework, you could go out and have fun, without unfinished work or a guilty conscience hanging over you.

In college, professors hand out syllabi on the first day of class that outline the semester's workload. Oftentimes, the grade you receive for a course depends only on a few exams and papers. Readings are assigned, but usually, there is no one to check up on you or quiz you to make sure you've done them in time—it is easy to get by without having done the reading for large lecture classes. It's also very easy to fall behind.

It is really up to you to keep up with the work. College is all about learning how to manage your time, to sit down and do the reading, knowing that it isn't due for a week, but that it is best to get started on 300 pages now. College is about realizing that often, you can't "finish" work—that there is always more to be done. (Actually, you find that in college, a lot of people spend an entire semester "catching up.")

It often comes down to decisions: Should I go out, even though it's Tuesday night, since I don't have to turn in anything for any of my classes tomorrow, or should I stay in and tackle the reading assignment I have for my comparative literature class? Learning how to manage your time is definitely an important part of your transition to college and really what marks the difference between high school and college. In college, you're on your own.

Logistical Nightmares

It can all seem pretty overwhelming: pass/fail, add/drop, waiting lists, and long lines at the registrar's office. It is. And not just for freshmen. The administrative side of college academics can be confusing and tangled and a source of great frustration for all students.

To get through it and get what you want, the most important thing is to understand all of the requirements before the class registration process actually begins. Many of these are outlined in your course catalogue, so read carefully. If you don't understand how a certain process works—e.g., how many days after class begins do you have to drop it—go the registrar's office and ask. No one is going to look at you as a stupid frosh, and if they do, who cares? You need to know things that have an impact on your courses and your grades.

Add/Drop

If you go to a few sessions of a certain class and hate it, consider switching. Just make sure that you'll be doing it for the right reasons and not simply because you got a poor grade on the first quiz. The add/drop process exists because sometimes we all make wrong choices, so don't think that you're doing something wrong by changing classes. Make sure to give each one a fair chance, think through your reasons for wanting to switch, consider if there are good alternatives, and then nail down the add/drop logistics to get through the experience smoothly.

Pass/Fail

Depending on your school, you'll be able to take a certain number of classes pass/fail. What this means is that no actual grade for the class will be recorded on your transcript or count toward your GPA. As long as you do well enough to pass— usually a "C" average, but do check with your school—that's the only evaluation that you'll receive. There are certainly benefits to taking a class pass/fail: You don't have to work as hard and don't risk a poor grade on your transcript. Taking a class pass/fail might make sense if you're taking an extremely challenging class and don't trust yourself to be able to do well in it.

But pass/fail has its negatives as well. It might look like you're taking your academics too easy and not challenging yourself enough. As with anything, moderation is key. Take a few classes pass/fail and it won't hurt you, and might even encourage you to take classes you wouldn't have taken for a grade. Pass/fail too many classes, and you're doing yourself a disfavor. Know your school's rules, consider your choices carefully, and make sure that you're always clear about timing—can you switch from taking a class pass/fail to a regular grade, and how much time from the beginning of class you have to do so.

Don't be overwhelmed by the logistics of choosing and taking classes. Know the requirements and stay in control by not missing deadlines.

Get What You Deserve

"Take the first semester seriously. Some students do not and find it difficult to then rebound their academic readiness as well as GPAs during subsequent semesters."

—Associate Director, Office of Admissions,
Purdue University

"If I hadn't gone to all of my Shakespeare lectures—even though some of them were a bit dull—I would have never known that the prof was obsessed with us quoting the texts in our term papers."

—Recent Grad, Wesleyan University

You're here to learn something. And while you'll learn a tremendous amount from just being on your own and interacting with all sorts of interesting people, you also want to get as much as you can out of your classes. You deserve it. You've worked to get here and it would be a shame if you spent hours a day in class without getting much out of it. (Plus, think of how much moola you and your family are paying for your education!)

Regardless of how brilliant your professors might be or how fascinating you find the class material, you'll need to put in some effort to get what you deserve—both in terms of your learning and your grades. Here are a few suggestions:

- **Go to class.** You can always find an excuse not to go: Your professor is boring, you can't understand his English, the material puts you to sleep, you're tired from partying late the night before, and so on. While it's certainly more than okay to skip class a few times—when you're sick, or have to get another life-or-death assignment in—try to not give in to the temptation too often. You'll learn more, meet more people, and have a chance to really get involved in the material.

There are also a few practical reasons to go to class. Some professors like to mark down attendance and take revenge against those who skip their class by grading them more strictly. Many professors talk about their exams and paper assignments in class, and mention what you'll need to study. You don't want to miss out on this info because it can really make a difference. Professors don't often come out and say exactly what you should study and exactly what your paper should be like, but if you pay attention, you'll learn a lot about each professor's preferences. We all have our quirks and they do, too.

Big introductory lectures have a tendency to be really boring. Hang in there and try to get what you can out of the class. You'll get a good overview of the particular academic discipline, which will make your choice of major easier later on. Also, these large classes are a good way to meet new people by forming a study group or griping about the boring lectures.

- **Study.** Find class material that is interesting and bite into it. This sounds like we're your parents or your teachers, but it's not bad advice. You're paying so much money for your education that it's a shame to just do the bare minimum and not get much out of your classes. And part of what we all do in college is figure out what interests us and what we might want to do after graduation—you never know if reading a really interesting psychology chapter might peak your interest in becoming a psychologist.

- **Find great profs.** Remember that amazing teacher who made your senior year statistics class the most exciting part of your year? Maybe not, but think of your favorite high school classes and, more likely than not, it was your teacher who made them that way. It's no different in college. Search out great profs and try to take a class with them. If your professor is engaging, knowledgeable, and enthusiastic about teaching, you'll learn a ton, even if the subject matter itself isn't particularly interesting.

"My professors are absolutely brilliant. They really motivate you to learn, and the amount of information that they can pass on is incredible—it's like they hold thirty books on one subject in their head."

—Freshman, Emory University

Word of mouth is a great way to learn about various professors and their teaching styles. Talk to some upperclassmen and see whom they recommend. Your resident advisor (RA) is another great resource.

- **Get to know your professors and help them to know you.** This can really take your college experience from okay to great, and we just wish that we figured that out during freshman year and not much later. Despite the obvious benefits of interacting with smart people—you can learn a tremendous amount and be inspired—knowing your professors can have positive practical results. Profs like students who care about the class and take the time to talk to them about it. If your professor likes you, he or she will be more inclined to give you higher grades.

If you plan on going on to grad school or applying to internships, you'll need recommendations from your professors. They can't write one unless they know you, so take the time and make the effort. Forming a friendship with a professor is really one of the best things about your college education. Great profs make all the difference.

Stay and chat after class. Go to a professor's office hours and talk about more than just the class or the assignments. Ask the professor about his or her areas of interest and what he or she is working on outside of class. Usually, professors are involved in research and writing academic articles, and they *love* to talk about themselves and their work.

Study Hall

"Try to get as much studying done between the hours of 8:00 am and 7:00 pm as possible. Don't put all of your learning off until late at night, because your retention is greatly decreased when the sun goes down."

—Assistant Dean of Students,
The College of William and Mary

In college you have lots more places, times, and ways to study than ever before. You have to find a way to study that works for you and allows you to get things done as well as possible and still leaves you time to do whatever it is you like to do outside of class.

First, find a place where you can get things done. Some of us do best locked up in our own room, minus the roommate and loud music. Some like to study in the library—seeing all of the books and heavy armchairs, hearing the muffled sounds of flipping

Study Tips
by Owen, Freshman, Emory University

The biggest of all study tips is to actually study! It's easy to go from high school, where you're constantly quizzed and constantly have assignments due, to college, where you're fairly unstructured academically, and lose all your motivation to study. One thing that makes studying easier for me is to go to the library—it takes me away from my computer, phone, TV, friends, and other distractions.

My advice is to try and set aside at least an hour every night to study no matter what. You can add on to this hour as exams and papers come up, but by studying at least an hour every night you're always staying on track. This way you won't go two weeks without doing any sociology work and then pick up the syllabus and realize that you only have two days to read a 600-page book.

The worst piece of advice I received was when a friend told me this: "Freshman year doesn't matter, man. Go out and party, don't go to class, it's not a huge deal because you're not taking serious classes anyway." As stupid as this sounds, I see a lot of college freshmen doing exactly what my friend told me to do.

In reality, many of your freshman classes do matter. Many of the professors you have your freshman year you will have again, and it helps a lot if they recognize you as a good student. And the attitude of "this doesn't matter" will not automatically switch off after your freshman year. If you don't take your freshman year seriously, you might find that it will be extremely hard to take your sophomore year seriously, and your junior year, and your senior year.

pages, and seeing everyone else be all academic and serious is not a bad inspiration to get to work. And when you need a break, there's always someone who could use one, too.

> "It was hard for me to work in my room. The littlest thing would distract me—whether it be people walking by or friends IMing me on the computer. If I was studying on my bed I'd lie down and fall asleep. It was so unproductive. I learned, however, that I could get my work done at the library. If all that's in front of me are my books on a nice, clean table, there's really nothing I can do besides study. Plus, seeing all the other people around me being studious and quiet motivates me to work hard as well."
>
> —Sophomore, Brown University

Everyone is different, and you just have to figure out where you'll do what type of studying best. Studying for an exam

 ## Allison's Corner

By the end of freshman year, I finally found a study system that worked for me. I can never read or work on my bed because it's too conducive to sleeping. I like to type papers in my room and read outside. Being outside, in the dorm or in a regular library room, means that there will be many social interruptions, so if I'm not pressed for time I'd rather take some breaks. If I need to take notes I go to our science library, but if I need to study hardcore, I go to the absolute-quiet room in the library and lock myself up for the night. I cannot learn before 11:00 am but retain most information when I stay up late and I'm in the "zone" of studying.

Procrastinators Beware!

Wasting time is easy. Email, Instant Messenger, computer games, video games, TV, the Internet, people playing outside or partying next door, downloading music, talking on the phone, and listening to music all seem like attractive distractions when you really can't seem to think of a good term-paper thesis. They can drag a two-hour reading assignment into a day's work.

We all procrastinate from time to time, and some of the best college moments, like a bonding talk with your roommate, happen because you're procrastinating. But you don't want to procrastinate too much—you'll waste a ton of time and leave yourself little room to relax and do things you really want to be doing. If you're a procrastination addict, try to work in an environment where it's more difficult to procrastinate—e.g., if you surf the Internet every chance you get, go somewhere where you can't access it when you study. Write out for yourself what you want to accomplish during each study period and keep the list somewhere close by. When you get the urge to procrastinate, look at your list and your watch.

If you're going to procrastinate, do something fun, relaxing, or productive. Talk to a friend, go for a run, read a nonclass book, go to an organizational meeting for a club you've been thinking about joining. Don't play computer games or be an Internet zombie; it will just make you more frustrated.

requires a laser-focused mind, so doing it out in the quad on a beautiful fall day might not be the most productive decision. Explore your campus—each has a few hidden treasures that are awesome study places.

Sometimes it might be helpful to study with a group from your class. You have a thought partner, someone to quiz you on the key points, and more than one mind to come up with good ideas and answers. Don't get addicted to study groups, though. They tend to become unproductive after too long.

Relearning Your ABCs

"In contrast to high school, where reading assignments took maybe half an hour at most, college assignments require large amounts of time and skimming skills. I often have to decide how much of the assignments to do, whereas in high school I was usually able to do every one."

—Junior, Yale University

You'll probably have more reading assigned for one of your college courses than you had for an entire semester of classes in high school. There will definitely be times when you get huge reading assignments and think: "I can't possibly read all of this in one or two nights!" Depending on what classes you take, the reading may also be very dense and difficult. It can certainly be very disheartening to spend several hours reading a dozen pages.

The key to getting through your reading is not to read like you usually do. What you have to master is the skill of reading for college. And that means that you have to have a plan of attack for each book or article, you have to prioritize certain sections over others, and you have to master the skimming technique. Here are some specific suggestions:

- **Pay attention in class.** Your professor will either explicitly say which sections of the reading are most critical or will emphasize certain parts of the material that you then should understand in detail. Many profs like to assign more reading than is humanly possible to complete, but paying close attention to what they focus on in class can help you prioritize.

- **Get an overall sense of the material.** It's hard to read page after page of dense material without having a general idea of where it's going. Before you dive into any reading material, look it over to get an idea of what topics it covers, how it's organized, and what sections relate most closely to what's being covered in class or to your paper assignment.

- **Read the introduction.** It's a road map to the source and it will give you a good idea of the points covered and the order in which they're covered.

- **Prioritize.** If you're working on a limited time schedule—and you're probably always working on a limited time schedule— find the most important sections of the material and read those first. There's nothing like showing up for the midterm and realizing that the two sections of the book that you never got to are the two sections that are core to the exam.

- **Take notes or highlight.** This is really key. Taking notes or highlighting the material in your books or handouts helps you remember it better. Don't try to write down every single point, but focus on the main thesis of each section and its important details.

- **Skim.** We don't know of many students who graduate from college without mastering the good old skill of skimming. There's no secret formula for how to skim, but you might want to read the introductory section or sentence, and then read the first few sentences of each paragraph. Skimming is a great way to get through the parts of your reading that are not central to what you're learning about.

You have to be careful, however, and pay close attention to what your professors emphasize in their paper assignments and exams. Some profs have quirks like asking questions about material that was in the footnotes of the reading. Try to get a sense of what these might be and read accordingly.

- **Mix it up.** Your mind will get tired if you try to read a hundred pages of dense philosophical writing all in one swoop. Give yourself a break, go outside for a few minutes, change the setting, and read somewhere else. Also, mix up what you're reading—do some for your econ class, some for history, some for psychology, etc.

"I went to a very small public school, and upon entering NYU, I felt like I was really far behind everyone else. People had read books that I'd never heard of, and I began to feel like I had slipped through the cracks somehow. I was just expected to know the stuff, or to work that much harder to catch up. It was quite an adjustment."

—Senior, New York University

Work Now, Sleep Later

"Buy a planner. University life, for many students, is the first time they are responsible for making sure they finish an assignment on time, make it to class on time, forecast busy times, etc. Be ready to get organized and use your daily planner to help you do it."

—Dean of Freshmen, Washington and Lee University

In high school, you were probably able to get all or most of your work done without much of a problem. In college, there's so much material to read and absorb, and papers and exams take longer to finish and study for. Sometimes it feels like you can hardly keep your head above this pool of work.

The only way to get through it is by mastering the art of prioritization. Some work is more important than other assignments, and you have to get it done first. For example, if you have a paper due tomorrow and a reading assignment for another class, you have to tackle the paper first and see how much time you have left for the reading.

Here are some tips that we've found useful:

- Buy one of those weekly planners and write down your assignments as soon as you get them. This will give you a good picture of what you have to get done and by when. You'll also see when there's an avalanche of work coming your way and be able to prepare by finishing up other assignments before then. If you know what you have to get done, it's much easier to prioritize your work.

"Most courses will have a syllabus that tells you when big papers and exams are coming up. This makes it easier for you to plan out your semester and know when your sleep time is about to dwindle."
—Recent Grad, Wesleyan University

- Try to at least glance at most of the reading you have to do. There's no need to read everything in detail—many professors like to assign hundreds of pages while only focusing on topics covered by a few. Figure out the most important parts of the reading, and skim through the rest.

Alarm Clock

by Jonathan, Junior, Wesleyan University

Beat this. I was teetering on the brink between a C+ and a B− in my freshman calculus class, so I really went the extra mile studying for the final. I did everything right: I began studying two weeks in advance, approached my professor with my slightest questions, and even got eight hours of sleep the night before! It was an evening exam, so I awoke bright eyed and bushy tailed, studied all day, and showed up to the exam room twenty minutes early. The room was empty and I felt good about arriving before anyone else. But an hour later, the classroom was still empty. I checked the online exam schedule and sure enough, the exam had been at 7:30 am, not 7:30 pm as I had thought. Forget a B−, I thought, I'm failing!

I emailed my professor who, as chance would have it, had slept through an alarm and missed an exam when he was a freshman. He gave me an incomplete and rescheduled the exam for after winter break. Although I hated studying over the vacation, I passed the class and learned several important lessons about how to succeed in college.

Write everything down! A planner costs less than five bucks at any drug store and can prove invaluable. If you don't think you need one, you're probably disorganized to begin with and need one all the more!

Also, going to office hours pays off. Even if some seem gruff, professors usually want to help you as much as they can. I could never have passed calculus without all the extra help during office hours, and I doubt my professor would have been as understanding about my missing the exam if he didn't already know me as a dedicated student.

- If you know in advance that there's just no way that you can get all of your "must do" assignments done on time, talk to your professors. Be reasonable and don't make this a habit, but explain your situation and ask for a modest extension. Not all profs are this kind, but some will give in.

Don't Fear Papers and Exams

The sheer number of papers and exams you'll have to tackle your freshman year can be pretty overwhelming. And unless you went to a private or ultra-competitive high school, chances are that you haven't had to write too many long research papers until now. Getting the hang of it and being able to write papers and prepare for exams in relatively short periods of time will be a challenge, but it's nothing you can't handle.

For exams, the key is to know what you have to study—what will be on the exam and what areas you're not so hot on. Find out as much as you can ahead of time by going to class, talking to the professor and TAs, and checking with your study group. Once you have a good idea of what will be covered, go over that material. Some of it you'll know cold, so you don't have to worry about studying it in detail. Some of it you'll need to work on more to brush up your memory. After you do an initial review, write down for yourself the key points to study and check them off as you do.

If your professor or TA holds a help session before an exam, definitely go. These can really help you to narrow down what will be on the exam and clarify what you need to study.

"I found final exams at college to be much, much more demanding than final exams at my high school. Primarily, the difficulty stems from the fact that college courses cover so much more material, and draw their questions from a much larger field of readings. At first, I had a lot of trouble figuring out what I most needed to know and then I'd become upset when I took an exam and realized that it did not cover most of the material I had been up the night before studying. After a semester or two, I began to realize how important it is to focus on studying the main topic of each lecture."

—Senior, Harvard University

Exams often account for a significant portion of your grade for the class, so put in some work here. Don't wait until the last minute to study, and make sure you know what's going to be on the exam.

College papers can be a challenge because they are longer than those you worked on in high school, require much more research and thought, and usually you have only a few weeks to write one. Don't panic, and try not to leave it to the last minute.

Below are a few general things you can do to help you with writing your college papers:

- **Develop a good thesis.** Regardless of the type of paper, you'll need to have a thesis, a main point that your paper will argue with supporting evidence. Make sure that you have one and that it's supportable and a bit original.

- **Approach research with a plan.** If you have to conduct research for your paper, don't dive into it without a plan.

Write down your preliminary thesis statement and a few supporting arguments you'd like to research. Use all of your library's resources and don't be shy to ask the librarians for help—they'll marvel at the chance to guide you. Keep track of your research using whatever method you like, but one that's consistent—write down the name of each source, the bibliographical information, the page number for the information you're taking down, and whether it's a direct quote.

- **Create a brief outline.** Don't waste hours upon hours writing out a super-detailed outline—you're better off writing the actual paper. Write down your thesis statement and the supporting arguments with a few data points for each. Use the outline to guide you through the paper, rather than overwhelm you with detail.

- **Write at least two drafts.** Even if you're a brilliant writer, print out and proofread your paper at least once. Spelling errors and bad grammar can really annoy some profs and bring down your grade. You deserve better, so make your paper free of errors you can avoid. And as you know already: Don't rely on the spell checker. Use it as the first step, but always double-check with your own eyes.

- **If you need an extension, ask early.** If there's no way in the world that you can get the paper done on time, ask for an extension. Not all profs will give it to you, but some might, and it doesn't hurt to ask. Exaggerating your tough circumstances is fine—you had three ridiculously difficult tests the same week the paper was assigned—but avoid making up colorful lies. They can usually see through them.

If you've left your paper assignment to the last minute, you're in the most popular club at college—the twenty-four-hour-paper club. Don't despair—it won't be fun, but you can still pull it off. Don't guzzle caffeine, but do develop a plan of action and pace yourself. Do all of the above steps, just quicker and with less thoroughness. And leave at least one hour at the end to print out and proofread the final draft.

 ## Katharine's Corner

I practically failed my first college midterm. After studying for weeks in advance, I took the test and thought I did pretty well. When we got our midterms back, much to my disappointment, I found myself at the bottom of the class. I thought to myself, "This is an intro psych class. Everyone here is taking psych for the first time. How could I score so badly compared to all these other first-timers?" Turns out there were a lot of upperclassmen taking it as an elective who knew how to study and how to get help.

After lots of tears, I finally went to my TA. To my surprise, I found her to be much more supportive and helpful than I had expected. She gave me some great tips on how to study for that specific type of test. I spent a good portion of my Christmas break studying for the final and wound up getting a decent grade in the class. I learned a lot about what works best for me in terms of study habits for that kind of subject matter. I also learned that a bad midterm grade does not have to mean doom for your overall grade in the class.

Have Hope

Even if you don't go to an ultra-difficult school, college academics can be pretty intense. Reading assignments are longer, papers are more frequent, and exams account for more of your grades than in high school. College academics can also be somewhat unpredictable, at least during your first few semesters. You have to adjust to new professors, each of whom has different demands and preferences, and each of whom grades differently.

Unless you're luckier than most, there will be moments when you feel discouraged—by your grades, by your seeming inability to do as well as you did in high school, or by the length of time it takes you to complete an assignment. It's completely and utterly

 A Note on Stress

College and stress are inseparable. You're trying to do a million things at once: meet new people, adjust to a completely new pace of life, do well in your classes, and still find time to socialize and get involved in extracurriculars. Phew! It can all get pretty stressful.

Some level of stress is completely normal, and you'll deal with it just fine. Find a few things that let your mind air out and chill out and make time to do them to keep yourself more or less sane. Go for a run, take a snack break, call up a friend, paint, do yoga, go to the gym—do whatever it is that takes your mind off of what's stressing you out. If you can, put things in perspective and help yourself see that a low grade on one of your exams is really not that huge of a deal and if you don't get that paper in on time, the world will not collapse.

understandable, and the first thing you should remember is that most of us have faced these moments of discouragement as well—you're not alone.

Don't let yourself get discouraged to the point where you give up trying. Do the opposite: Use these moments to fire yourself up and do better and work harder. You'll feel pretty great when you overcome your academic challenges and your feelings will be much more rewarding than if everything came easily.

If you're not happy with your grades and feel like you're doing all you can without success, talk to your professor and your academic advisor. They might be able to point out areas for you to focus on, and it will generally be helpful to talk these things through. Don't go in whining about your lower-than-you-think-you-deserve grades. Rather, explain that you're working hard and seem to be unable to get higher grades, and ask for feedback and suggestions.

There might be times when you get extremely stressed and anxious. You can't sleep, you're eating badly or not at all, you

Allison's Corner

While I'm a pretty laid-back person, I can get caught up in the pressure of getting good grades. A couple of things I've done to relieve stress this year are practicing yoga or going for a run. I take food breaks or watch some trashy television such as *Real World*. Sometimes I take full days off just to unwind and not do anything. Although this can put me behind in work, a mental-health day can revitalize me for delving into the future reading.

Comic Relief: *Lessons*
by Jay, Junior, Columbia University

In college, free with the price of admission are many extracurricular lessons. You'll learn to live on your own and navigate through bureaucracy; maybe you'll learn to cook or how much alcohol you can drink before prank calling your professors seems like a good idea. I learned how to raise the hem of my pants and that even though fabric softener and laundry detergent come in similarly shaped bottles, they don't serve the same purpose.

Here's a story about the most important thing I learned in college: Pay close attention so you don't have to learn it the way I did or, worse yet, teach it to others.

Instead of the usual lecture, we were going to watch a video in class. Everybody was expecting a documentary, or maybe something broadcast on public television from a few decades ago. The teacher put the tape in the VCR and pressed play, and it took a second to register that we were watching homemade porn! Though she immediately shut it off, it took about ten minutes before the laughter in the room quieted down to the point where the mortified teacher could tell us about her boyfriend's impending death. "I don't approve of such things," she said, "and our VCR was broken, so I didn't preview it."

Which leads me to the moral of the story and the most important thing I've learned in college: Always double-check.

don't seem to be able to focus, and your mind is spinning in ten different directions. You might need to talk to someone to get out of the stress cycle. Consider going to a counselor at your school or talking to your parents—this is what they're really great for.

Can You Help Me?

"Be assertive: You need to reach out, you need to be your own advocate, you need to ask questions, you need to meet people different from yourself, you need to get to know at least one staff member or faculty member, and all of that starts by being assertive."

—Vice Chancellor for Student Affairs and
Dean of Students, Indiana University

It's not embarrassing to use the advising resources provided for you on campus. It's smart. Many of us don't ask for help because we feel that it makes us look stupid. We think now that we're in college, we're supposed to figure things out on our own. Well, that's not true at all. We're at college to learn and do it with the help of our professors, advisors, tutors, and other students. Why would all of the campus resources be around if we weren't supposed to use them?

Ironically, professors tend to think more highly of students who ask for advice and help because they're really challenging themselves to understand the material. If you feel like you need help, don't wait—go and talk to your professor. You'll save yourself a lot of frustration and help improve your grades.

"I realized during my sophomore year that many profs relate better to students who try, fail, and then try again than students who get it on the first try. No one is expecting you to be perfect, and many professors will be more than willing to help you out if you show initiative."

—Recent Grad, Wesleyan University

Another great resource is your academic advisor. You will probably be assigned one at the beginning of the year, or you might be able to choose one. Meet with your advisor as you choose your classes—it's great to have someone to bounce ideas off. Your advisor might also be helpful as you confront various college issues, whether social or academic. Don't ignore this person as the year goes on—it's always good to have someone who is not your professor or your friend to talk to about things.

If you don't like your advisor or don't seem to get along, see if there is a way you can switch. Having someone whom you can talk with is important, and you should feel comfortable with that person.

Try to meet with your dean at least once during first semester. Deans can be great to help with organizing your schedule and dealing with sometimes complicated academic logistics. Their job is talk to students, so help them do it by stopping by.

If tutoring is available on your campus, take advantage of it. It's not embarrassing to get help early on; it can prevent future damage and help you do really well in a class. If you didn't need help in high school, it doesn't mean you're stupid now to ask. It means that you've matured and are learning some pretty advanced stuff.

Another great resource are your TAs. Most of your professors will have an upperclassman or a graduate student working with them. TAs do everything from grading papers and exams to holding study sessions and prep sessions for tests—they generally know the class material well and can shed some light on the professor's quirks and pet peeves. Get to know your TAs. Talk to them if you have a question and go to a few study sessions to see if they're helpful.

Too Much of a Good Thing
by Adam, Junior, Columbia University

When I first came to college, I thought I was so tough. I boasted of never getting sick and considered myself the Bruce Lee of sleep deprivation. I was determined to work and play harder than any other student on campus. I spent so many hours in the library studying for my first finals that I brought a change of clothes and a toothbrush along. I endured this hellish experience by dreaming of winter break. When my last exam finally ended and I returned home for vacation, I immediately came down with the flu. So much for my break.

Instead of learning from this, I worked just as hard at the end of the spring term. This time my body gave an even clearer signal that I was working too hard—I got pneumonia days before my first exam. I was too feverish to see the lines on the bluebook page, so I had to take incompletes in several classes. Worst of all, I was alone in my dorm room without Mom to carry bowls of chicken noodle soup and cold glasses of ginger ale to me in bed.

Don't work too hard! In the first place, it's counterproductive—my grades suffered from my Rambo-like study skills. More important, there is a lot of worth studying in college *outside* of that dreary library. Be sure to study, but take your toothbrush on more interesting trips than to the stacks!

"TAs are a huge resource! They do much of the grading and often know exactly what professors look for in papers."

—Senior, Columbia University

Find out if your college has a writing workshop and use this invaluable resource when you're working on a paper. Meet with a writing tutor to talk about your ideas for how to structure a paper, to get help after you've written the first draft, or when you need an independent pair of eyes to proofread your work. Writing tutors are usually students who are great writers, and you'll feel very comfortable talking to them.

> "My writing abilities were not at the level my English professor expected, and he wasn't enthusiastic to help me either. The writing center proved to be extremely helpful. I firmly believe that the three hours I spent there helped raise my grade considerably."
>
> —Freshman, Emory University

5

After-Class Fun

College is a great time to try something new, both inside and outside the classroom. There are endless opportunities to get involved in clubs, organizations, teams, and activities, and you have a chance to try out things that you've never done before. Take the time to explore your options and get involved in a few activities you really enjoy. Don't worry about making your resume look good. If you do what you like and care about, everything else will fall into place.

There's no downside to getting involved in some extracurriculars: You'll learn new things, make new friends, and have a much more diverse and interesting college experience. Just be careful not to go overboard. If your grades are slipping, you get no sleep, and spend most of your free time running from one meeting to another, consider the possibility that you're doing too much.

- Your Own Box of Chocolates
- Nothing to Lose
- Sports Stardom
- It's Your Life
- Don't Go Overboard

Your Own Box of Chocolates

"It's important to become deeply engaged in activities and programs—both on and off campus—in the city and region in which you reside during your freshman year. The quality of your experience is immeasurably enhanced by being engaged in your community."

—Vice Provost for University Life,
University of Pennsylvania

Even if you go to a small college, there is probably a ton of things you could do outside of class. Varsity and intramural sports, theater, college newspapers, volunteer organizations, student government—the list goes on and can be a bit mind-boggling. Take the time to explore all of your options and keep your mind open for new things you might not have considered.

Before you come to school, you can do a bit of research to see what activities are available. Check out your college's website—it usually has an area dedicated to student activities.

There's also usually an activities fair at the beginning of each academic year. Go! Grab your roommate and check it out. You don't have to commit to anything right away—just talk to the students from the organizations that interest you, get their intro materials, and think it over.

"I found new friends not through parties but through the extra-curriculars I participate in. That's what's so wonderful about a school like this—almost everyone has something interesting to offer. And I realize that I, too, fit into this scheme."

—Sophomore, Brown University

Remember that there might be things to do off campus as well, like tutoring at a local high school or writing for the local paper, for example. If you think you might be interested in getting involved in something off campus, check around—sometimes the career and financial aid centers will have information on these activities.

Once you've found a few things you're interested in, go to a meeting or two and see what the people are like. With whom you'll be spending your time is pretty much as important as what you'll be doing, and the only way to find out is by meeting other participants.

"In high school I was a huge fish in a very small pond. I did every-thing and did it well. When I got to college, I found out that about 500 other students had done everything that I did in high school and more. I realized that I was suddenly a tiny guppy in a very large ocean of sharks. It was very intimidating to even consider joining clubs, so I just didn't. Looking back, it's something I really regret. I wish I made that much more of an effort to distinguish myself in college."

—Senior, New York University

To Be or Not to Be . . . Greek?

"After making friends with people who were in frats, I realized that there really isn't one 'typical frat boy,' despite the stereotypes. I shouldn't have judged this group so quickly."

—Junior, University of Pennsylvania

"My advice would be to not rush too early in the year because then you might limit your group of friends. And if you join, definitely make friends outside of your Greek organization."

—Sophomore, The College of William & Mary

Some campuses don't have a single fraternity or sorority, others are completely dominated by them. Like with any other activity—and this one can be much more life consuming—explore your options before deciding to join. Make sure you're not doing it just because all of your friends are. Being part of a fraternity or a sorority can be an intense experience, and you have to want it.

Greek organizations are often big into community service, are a great way to meet people and create a community, during and after college, and are always having parties. Some even offer great housing that's ten times better than what you could hope for in the dorms.

But frats and sororities can also be quite limiting on your social life and can consume much of your free time. Hazing, depending on the campus, can be scary. People really are beaten with paddles and ordered to swallow goldfish. "Rushing" Greek institutions means a lot of socializing and gabbing superficially with people you want to like you, and pledging can mean getting up in the middle of the night to scrub the house with a toothbrush after a party.

Nothing to Lose

College is a time to take risks and branch out to discover what you're passionate about. It's not the time to be safe by sticking to what you're good at. Try new things! If you were too self-conscious in high school to try out for the play, take a chance now and do it. Never thought of playing a team sport? Join an intramural team—it can be great fun without being ultra-competitive. If you like juggling, go juggle in front of the library or start your own club for *Saved by the Bell* lovers.

When you come to college, you have this great chance to shed the shackles of what's in your past and start fresh. No one knows the old you, and no one cares. You can like and do new things without worrying about creating or supporting some kind of an image of yourself.

 Katharine's Corner

My main activity in high school was performing. When an injury sidelined me from the dance studio for an entire year, I was devastated. I'd spent my entire life dancing, and now the idea of facing a semester with no dance was absolutely horrifying. I joined the gospel choir in an effort to fill the void in my schedule and found it to be the most rewarding decision I'd made at school. After overcoming the injury, I'm back in the dance studio, but now I have a whole new set of interests and friends that I never would have gained without that injury.

Try things you've never considered. When else if not now? The worst thing that can happen is that you'll absolutely hate it and swear to never, ever do it again. But that's much better than graduating and thinking: "I wish I'd done [fill in activity here] when I had the chance." The real world—or whatever you want to call the world after college—is pretty hectic, and your time to do fun things outside of work is so much more limited. You have it now, so use it!

Sports Stardom

"Joining the Frisbee team was the best thing I've done so far socially at school. I made a second set of friends outside of the dorm and was able to avoid dorm drama (drama defined as what happens when people live in close proximity to each other and hang out too much). The camaraderie and built-in social scene made it easy to fit in. Traveling, exercising, and seeing new places with friends is fun!"

—Sophomore, University of Delaware

Getting involved in sports at college can be a very rewarding experience—a great group of friends, stress relief, fun exercise— and you can choose to what degree you're involved. There are four main ways to play sports at college: varsity, clubs, intramural, and pickup.

Basically, they break down like this:

- Varsity sports are for intercollegiate athletes and those who played competitive sports all through high school. Some athletes may have been recruited to play for your school.

This group of athletes is rather elite, and you'll most likely be a fan of these students as opposed to a teammate. Some schools hold open tryouts for their varsity squads, but many don't—it depends on the size of your school. Varsity sports are a serious time commitment, so before you sign up, make sure you have the time and the will to tackle them.

- Club teams play other colleges, but they're much less rigorous than varsity, often without a full-time coach or with a student who serves as the coach. Depending on the size of your school, the number of club teams will range from two or three to several dozen. Club teams will let you be competitive without the serious commitments of varsity, and while you may not have to try out, you will spend time traveling to other colleges.

- Intramural sports are organized leagues within your school where students create their own teams and compete against each other. We highly recommend that you join any and all intramural leagues in which you enjoy playing the sport because the level of fun greatly outweighs any time constraints (and you can always skip games without too many repercussions, other than your friends' nagging).

- And if you just don't feel like being part of any organized team, for many team sports you can usually find a bunch of students playing pickup, especially for sports like basketball, Ultimate Frisbee, or volleyball.

While you may think that you know how you want to get involved in college-level sports, take a chance and stretch your abilities. Go to an open tryout, and you might surprise yourself.

If you have the time to commit, you may be able to make the varsity swim team even if you only competed for two years in high school. All you need to do is take the initiative.

It's Your Life

"At an interview for a summer internship, my interviewer asked me about working for the international students' newspaper, an activity I listed on my résumé. I really didn't have a great time with this organization and as I tried to fake enthusiasm, the interviewer asked why I didn't just quit if I clearly wasn't into it. It wasn't a good moment."

—Recent Grad, Wesleyan University

Your time is a precious commodity, so make sure that you get involved in activities because you want to and not because you think you should or because they'll make your résumé look better. If you're passionate about what you're doing, you're usually better at it and much happier. Seriously. If you love something and do it with energy, it will look good on you and your résumé.

Your future employers—including internships and summer jobs for which you might apply during school—don't care about the sheer number of activities in which you're involved. They care about how those activities help you learn, mature, and express yourself. When you go to interviews, you'll probably be asked about your college extracurriculars. If you're not really excited about them, it's pretty easy to spot. And it is your passion and excitement about what you do that your future employer really does care about.

Do stuff that you like. It will make your life so much better and will help to relieve much of the stress that's so prevalent during college.

Don't Go Overboard

Don't go crazy with activities your freshman year, and particularly during the first semester. You need time to adjust, to make new friends, and to figure out how much of your days will be filled with studying. Not getting involved in a ton of activities right away won't hurt you—they'll still be there later.

When deciding in which activities to get involved, keep in mind how much time each will require. College sports can be extremely time consuming, so be careful what else you plan to do during the particular sports season. And if you're involved in a play, it usually takes up most of your free time, so perhaps put off all other activities until later. Be realistic.

The academic/extracurricular/social balance is also very important. What consumes most of your time will vary, depending on factors such as an impending midterm or hellish tech week schedule for a theater performance. In general, we suggest roughly a 40/30/30 split in terms of time spent on academics, extracurriculars, and your social/personal life. Obviously there's no precise formula for how to organize your time, but just recognize that college is about more than just one thing or activity.

If you feel overwhelmed with numerous extracurriculars, you're probably doing too much. Don't feel like a loser who can't handle it and instead remember that you're in a new atmosphere with tougher requirements. Everyone needs some breathing room.

Chocolates

by Rachel, Sophomore, Brown University

College is like a box of chocolates: You want to sample one of everything, but try too many and you'll get sick! I could scarcely say no to an extracurricular activity when I first came to school. "Actually, I'd love to join; I've always wanted to learn how to rock climb. Student Aeronautics Association, what's that? Sure I'll join it if I really get to fly a plane every weekend. The blowfish cooking club? Sounds great!" I made *Rushmore*'s Max Fisher look like a recluse.

I'd stagger into a club meeting exhausted from class, home-work, and work-study, and expect to have the time of my life. Instead, I found cold pizza, name games, and an offer to attend the more serious organizational meeting next week. I didn't real-ize that to enjoy an extracurricular, you have to invest the time to learn the ropes and earn the seniority necessary to actively participate in it. The more novel the activity, the more time it requires.

Savor your college chocolates by focusing on one extracurricu-lar in your first semester. Maybe try two, but you won't have the time to develop any one interest if you try too many. Needless to say, your grades and social life may also suffer. I know how hard it can be to balance enthusiasm with pragmatics, but don't waste your precious first weeks of college running from quilting club to lightweight sumo wrestling tryouts like I did!

"The first year can be tough just because it's a lifestyle change. You're living in a different place, in a different way, with different people. It can be difficult to maintain the gung-ho attitude that most of us had in high school when the base parts of your life have been switched around. Who wants to worry about auditioning for a student group or taking on extra credit when you still haven't gotten the hang of the laundromat?"

—Senior, Stanford University

Don't neglect free time to hang out with friends, go to the gym, read outside, and just generally chill out. You need to leave room for relaxing in your schedule or you risk missing out on the benefits of socializing with other students, and may burn out.

If you do get involved in too many activities, be smart enough to realize it and don't feel guilty for dropping a few. Do this before your grades slip and your sleep time is reduced to two hours a night.

6

Getting a Social Life

No, no, we're not that book about college that pretends that college is just about studying hard and making sure that you and your roommate don't kill each other. (Although we do think that both are quite important.) College wouldn't be college if it didn't come packed with all kinds of parties and entertainment.

Having fun with new people with few real cares in the world is why it's pretty great to be eighteen. All of us like different things and have fun in different ways—wherever you go to school, you will definitely find other people who like to do what you do and do it together. You might not find your groove right away, but it will happen.

But as you're having a blast, be smart. Your newly found freedom comes with huge potential risks, and it's totally up to you to stay out of trouble. Here are a few suggestions for how to enjoy this freedom without losing your mind, your college education, or your life.

Everyone Needs a (Social) Life

"Balancing your social life and your academics means sometimes putting your social life first."

—Senior, Harvard University

Adjusting to college isn't easy, regardless of what type of high school you attended. You're going to miss the friends you grew up with. Even if you weren't that social in high school, you still lived at home, surrounded by your family, and someone was there to keep an eye on you. You may have also had friends or neighbors who watched you grow up and were always around.

At college, you're without your old network of parents, friends, and acquaintances. Unless you're extraordinarily independent, the only way to survive is to develop a college "family" in the form of your friends. It's important to put some effort into making friends and creating a supportive circle of peers and advisors.

As we've said before: Do what makes you comfortable. Get out there, meet new people, make new friends, but know when to give yourself a break and take time for yourself. You don't need to know the entire campus—a close-knit group of a few friends is what you may cherish most.

W.W.F. Wrestling—Penn Style
by Sujit, Senior, University of Pennsylvania

When I first got to school, I spent my free nights in one of two ways: I'd follow a freshman flock to a frat party, or on weekday nights, I'd scan the flyers littering the dorms for a freshman ice-breaker. I first enjoyed meeting new people at these gatherings, but Trivial Pursuit tournaments gradually lost their luster and the company began to seem as stale as the food. Where had all the interesting freshmen gone, I wondered? To the *interesting* events on campus, that's where.

You have to look away from postings in elevators and restroom mirrors to find some of the greatest opportunities on campus. Don't rely on the emails the dean sends to every freshman to find events. Scan department bulletin boards on your way to class and ask upperclassmen to forward you the emails they receive from student clubs, museums, or local music venues. If your school borders a big city, subscribe to *Time Out* magazine. Foreign language departments and student film societies screen all kinds of movies, from silent Polish art films to blockbusters. Always drop by art exhibits and author readings. If the artists disappoint you, console yourself with the free wine.

Pedantic as it sounds, I love the evening lectures Penn offers. They feature specialists in any field you're interested in and who are often famous and almost always entertaining. This was really brought home to me when I saw Alan Dershowitz debate Alan Keyes at the law school. If you're imagining two crusty academics bantering in phony British accents, think again! I'd never seen such animated—or for that matter, intelligent—speakers in my life! I felt like I was watching a W.W.F. fight break out at Socrates's School of Athens!

Find Your Own Groove

"Take care with alcohol, drugs, and sex. College is a time of experimentation, but you'll be happier if you exercise some degree of self-discipline and common sense. You will be more in control, and, in some situations, that will be key to your personal safety."

—Dean of Student Affairs, Bowdoin College

Having a great time one night and drinking too much will give you a severe hangover, but it won't impact your life dramatically. Drinking too much every weekend will get you everything from alcohol poisoning and depression to poor grades and possibly an expulsion from school.

As with so much else, balance and moderation is what you're after. Whatever it is that you choose to do with your free time, don't overdo it and know when to stop. It's great to be on your own and without your parents watching your every step. But it also means that you have to watch your own steps and know when you're headed in the wrong direction.

"College is all about choices. You could sleep late, or come to class. You could have an alcoholic beverage, or stay sober. You could write a paper before it's due, or you could rush to get it done. Make the decisions that you think are right."

—Sophomore, Quinnipiac University

We've All Been Here

"Always keep your goals in sight. The freedom that comes with the transition from high school to college can be very seductive. Students sometimes make choices in the excitement of the moment that jeopardize their long-range plans. College should be an enjoyable experience; however, its primary purpose is not to entertain but to help you mature, both intellectually and socially."

—First-Year Student Coordinator, Deans' Office,
Ursinus College

You might have partied a ton in high school. Or maybe you're drinking your first beer in college. Regardless, know that drinking can turn all shades of ugly and know that you do have the responsibility to prevent yourself from getting into those ugly situations.

Before we go anywhere else, two reminders that you should etch deeply into your mind: *Never, ever, ever drink and drive,* and *don't mix drugs and alcohol.* Take a moment and read those words over a few more times.

Now that the really serious stuff is out of the way, here are a few other issues to watch out for:

Freshman Freedom Syndrome

Problem:

Without Mom and Dad, you're free at last to eat, drink, and party to excess. Without rules, it's easy to go crazy and exploit your freedom. However, too many of us have suffered from the inability to control our overexcitement. When schoolwork slacks off, grades drop, and you can't remember much about your days except for partying and drinking, you know you've gone too far.

Solution:
While it's good to enjoy your freedom, don't be stupid and abuse it. That will only mean trouble for you with the school, your parents, and your life. Set up some restrictions for yourself—e.g., not going out more than two times a week—and try to calm down. You have four years to have fun and don't need to cram it all into your first two semesters. If you do realize that you've let your life outside of partying slip away, don't despair. You made the mistake early on and have more than three years in which to fix it.

> "If you're going to make a mistake, make it early on in freshman year so that you can blame it on your adjustment to college. It's easy to get overenthusiastic and begin abusing your fun time, but sadly enough it all catches up to you by mid-semester."
>
> —Sophomore, Brown University

Getting Caught

Problem:
If you're under twenty-one, drinking alcohol is undeniably illegal. Most schools adopt a pretty realistic attitude about students drinking and care much more about your safety than strictly upholding the law. Not all are so kind, however, and you can get busted at a party—and certainly at the local pub.

Solution:
Be discreet. Don't run around campus screaming with a can of beer in your hand. If you're having a party in your room, close

the door and windows. If you're at a party and campus police are coming to check IDs, try to get rid of your alcohol as quickly as you can and without making a fuss. And if you get caught, don't try to lie—it's too easy to check how old you are. Apologize, look sorry, and beg.

Can't-Go-to-Class Hangover

Problem:
After a night of drinking more than you should have, your body is dehydrated, exhausted, and shocked by the sudden lack of alcohol. Your head hurts, your stomach aches, and if you just crack your eyes open a little, your head starts to spin. There is no way in the world that you can make it to your morning class.

Solution:
A good rule of thumb is to drink one cup of water for every beer you consume. If this is impossible, gulp down as much water as you can before you go to bed. This prevents the dehydration that causes many of your symptoms. Drink a ton of water when you wake up as well. If you truly feel awful, close the shades, and go to sleep to give your body some rest. Later call up the professor whose class you missed, apologize profusely, explain that you were sick, and ask what you need to make up.

Beer Goggles

Problem:
After a few drinks anyone can look hot, and there's a chance that you end up kissing someone to whom you wouldn't go close if

you were sober. Worse, you could leave the party with a stranger or a friend who is not a friend—and you could end up getting hurt, physically and emotionally.

Solution:
Try not to drink so that your vision blurs, literally and figuratively. Make a plan before you go out about what you will and will not do and what your drinking limit is. Remember that you drink to chill out and not to freeze your judgment. If you're ever in a shady situation, immediately stop drinking and find a way to leave with someone you trust. Bring a party buddy who will look after you if you lose your senses.

Alcohol Poisoning

Problem:
You drink so much that your body can't process and rid itself of the alcohol and its toxins from your blood stream. You become severely ill, dehydrated, throw up, and pass out. In the worst situations, you stop being able to breathe. This is really scary stuff and it's life threatening. If it ever happens to you, hope that there is a responsible friend nearby. And if you ever see someone in this condition, become that responsible friend.

Solution:
Don't drink past your limit. Binge drinking is extremely stupid and dangerous, and you should never, ever have the need to go there. If you do drink, supposedly you do it because it helps you chill out a bit and relax. No way in the world should you need to relax to the point of risking your life. Keep track of how many

drinks you have and stop yourself from reaching for yet another one. If you feel that you can't control yourself, ask a trusted friend to help you. And if you ever see someone drinking too much or in a condition where it's clear that he or she needs medical help, get it. This is no time to worry about the person getting in trouble with the school—you need to save his or her life. Call an ambulance and the campus police.

Alcohol Abuse

Problem:
Your schoolwork is slipping because you've been out boozing every night this week. You're wasted all weekend and can barely remember what happened. Your friends ask you to drink less because you get too out of control.

Solution:
Recognize that this is a problem and seek help from friends, counselors, and parents. Alcohol abuse and alcoholism are serious medical problems and you can't cure them on your own. No one will blame you for getting out of control, but they will help you. It's sad, but hundreds of college students binge drink and abuse alcohol, and too many of them end up ill for life or with no life at all. Don't be them; get help.

Don't Be Naïve About Drugs

Taking drugs is illegal. There, we've said our adult bit. But as with much else, everyone in college makes a personal choice

D.A.R.E.

by Nathaniel, Junior, Columbia University

Consider the following riddle: What shows strangers what's beneath its clothes and then shows friends what's inside its stomach? Answer: a college student who doesn't know how to drink.

At any party you can spot the freshmen whose parents sheltered them from all knowledge of sex, liquor, drugs, and other dangers in high school, only to turn them loose in college without any understanding of limits. These students go to their first party and end up in a stranger's room or, worse, a hospital bed. I don't blame these students. After all, I was one of them once.

My parents kept close tabs on me, and where they couldn't follow me, their network of informers did. In a small town like the one I grew up in, you simply don't have the freedom to break the rules and, as a consequence, you never learn to set them for yourself. I had to write a couple papers Sunday morning with earsplitting headaches in order to learn how to respect alcohol. Some people aren't so lucky. Try having to explain a $500 ambulance ride to your parents after campus police decide you need your stomach pumped. I have a friend who got kicked out of his dorm for smoking pot. He couldn't afford an apartment so he had to withdraw for a semester, which this hurt his chances of getting into medical school.

As a not-so-proud D.A.R.E. graduate, I know that scare tactics don't work. I think we're old enough to make our own decisions, but this isn't as simple as it sounds—it means thinking about what you're doing and seriously considering the consequences.

about drug use—whether to do it at all and, if yes, what drugs to use. You should never forget that you do have the choice and that nothing is cooler than the choice that seems right for you.

Taking some drugs can be addictive and sometimes dangerous. Missing classes, failing tests, avoiding friends, and losing tons of money on a drug habit is not cool and can quickly cause you to drop out of college. Getting caught with illegal drugs can result in disciplinary consequences, ranging from warnings to expulsions. Don't be naïve, and never forget that the choices you make will affect your life.

If you do decide to use drugs, be extremely careful that you know what you're doing and where what you're about to put into your body is coming from. Seriously. Not everyone means well, and unless you can have some degree of confidence in knowing what you're about to consume, don't do it. You don't have to trust anyone but yourself, and you don't have to look cool for anyone else's sake. If something looks suspicious, it is.

Know that if you're going to take a drug once, there is an extremely high chance that you will do it again. Ecstasy is infamous for its ability to overcome even the strictest of promises to never try it again. Drugs can be more powerful than your will, and you should have no illusions about that.

And never mix drugs and alcohol. Your body shouldn't have to handle that amount of toxic stress all at once.

If you feel at any point that your drug use is out of control, get help. Don't try to fight the problem all on your own; know that help is there. Check if your school has a special hotline or a counselor at the health center.

More than Meets the Eye

"Be picky. Not every party is a good one."

—Freshman, Brown University

On any given weekend, there are tons of parties and other social activities going on at college. Take some time to explore what they are and find the atmosphere that you enjoy the most. If you're sick of going to the same loud, beer-drinking party every weekend, suggest to your friends to try that open-mike night that you've been wondering about. If you find that your friends always want to do the same thing on weekends, you might have to take the initiative and find a new group to do something different with from time to time.

It's much easier to change your social circle, your friends, and what you do with your free time during freshman year, when everyone is still figuring out how they fit into this new college experience, than later on. Take advantage of this and try as many different things and hang out with as many different people as possible.

"I'm a shy person, and people tell me now that they used to think I was a snob. It doesn't matter if you know what you're like, though, you have to show other people, too. I wish I'd taken more risks in terms of going out with new people and taking initiative to introduce myself."

—Sophomore, Middlebury College

First Impressions

by Catherine, Sophomore, University of Delaware

The first weekend I went out, I played the standard freshman role of walking around campus with just about everyone on my floor, following people who had vaguely heard through friends of friends of friends where the parties were. It was exciting, thinking how I was at college, going out, meeting people who could potentially become good friends of mine. The most exciting thing was knowing that I didn't have to explain to my parents where I was going, who with, or what time I'd be home!

One Saturday night I found myself slowly being pushed to the outskirts of the room by people waiting on the endless line for the keg. The people with whom I had come were playing a drinking game of sorts in which I wasn't interested, and no one else at the party seemed to even notice my existence. I suddenly felt as though I was surrounded by people with whom I didn't have much in common. Fighting back tears, I ran home convinced I would never feel at home at school.

Soon after that first shaky experience, I started to love being at college. During the first couple of weeks it's very easy to obtain a warped sense of what your school is like. Judging from my first time out, I would have thought that I would hate being here, but I found out that there's so much more out there than frat parties and anonymous drunkenness—there are a million activities, and there are people who are interested in meeting you and hearing what you have to say.

Don't become jaded or disillusioned by your school too fast. Give it a fair chance.

Escape the Campus Bubble

Whether your university happens to be in a bustling metropolis or a quaint little college town, the local community can offer an interesting and pleasant escape from the campus social scene. If there are other universities in the area, the city can be a good place to meet a wider range of people. No matter how big your campus is, or how full it is of things to do, an occasional change of scenery can provide a much-needed break from your usual routine.

Grab a few friends and go exploring. Seek out a funky little café, go dancing at a club, find an interesting theater performance—just do something different. Life on campus can sometimes begin to feel like you live in a bubble. Get some air.

Watch Your Wallet

A college campus is probably one of the only places where you can have a great time and do a ton of different things on a tight budget.

But if your college is close to a city filled with exciting entertainment or shopping opportunities, watch out! Between hefty cover charges, overpriced food or drinks, and expensive taxis back to campus after public transportation has stopped running, a night of being out and about can get expensive, and a few too many nights or days like that can get your bank account into serious trouble.

When it comes to activities such as dinner at a nice restaurant or going to expensive clubs, you might feel a bit awkward that some of your classmates seem to have money to throw around while you're living on a tight budget. It's easy to get lured into spending more money than you should simply because that's what your friends are doing and you want to be part of the fun. We've definitely all been there.

You know your limits. Don't spend money you don't have just for the sake of not feeling left out. The majority of your fellow classmates are on tight budgets and don't have much extra cash. If your friends want to eat out, there's nothing wrong with suggesting an inexpensive restaurant. Have fun, go out, but know when you need to politely say no to doing something with your friends or to suggest that you all do something less expensive.

7

Navigating
the Dating Maze

Whether you're a serial dater, have had the same significant other for the past four years, or have never much gotten into dating, the college dating scene will probably not be much of what you've experienced before. When you see the guy you broke up with in the bathroom every morning or the girl whom you haven't called in weeks is your new chemistry TA, things can get pretty interesting.

It's nothing you can't handle, but here are a couple things to think about.

- No Strings Attached
- The Walk of Shame
- Let's Talk About Sex
- Don't Joke About It

No Strings Attached

"It was strange just to cut off my romantic relationship at home because I was leaving for college. Honestly, it seemed wrong, and I couldn't understand why people were advising me to do it. Now, I can't imagine I would have had such a great year if I was still attached to someone at home."

—Sophomore, Chaminade University

Some of us come to college with a significant other from home who is at a different school and beginning a different life. We promise ourselves that the relationship is important and we can make it work. And for the first few days on campus we hang on the phone for hours, crying our eyes out to the familiar ear on the other end.

But it's not always easy to keep a long-distance relationship going and not necessarily something that you should try to do during your freshman year. Continuing a high school relationship means enormous phone bills, sappy email love letters, and always having to miss someone. Although some couples pull it off, it's hard to resist the temptations that college offers you and difficult to maintain a close connection while both of you are changing with your new settings.

Don't force yourself to keep an old relationship going or think that you're a bad person for breaking it off—your significant other might have the same thoughts but not know how to go about acting on them. Unless you're absolutely positively crazy in love, both of you will benefit from having the freedom to grow and explore relationships with new people. By constantly leaving campus to visit your love interest, you may miss out on your university's life. You'll miss meeting new people, which is especially important freshman year when it's easier to make friends. Most high school sweethearts break up sometime during freshman year, so don't be crushed and recognize that this is your opportunity to grow.

If you do decide to stick it out and stay together, be realistic. Set some rules about phone calls and visits that will allow you both to get immersed into your new college lives. Don't spend every Friday night stuck in the library exchanging Instant Messages with your boyfriend or girlfriend—it's not romantic.

The Walk of Shame

"Don't jump into things. You have four years—you don't need to hook up with someone tomorrow."

—Freshman, Brown University

Staying out of dating-related trouble at college requires a bit more finesse than in high school. The same person you mistakenly kissed last night might be sitting next to you in class the next morning. And your ex from first semester might end up as your writing workshop tutor during the second.

The key is to be respectful and extra careful about what you say to whom. Even huge campuses have an amazing speed of dating information exchange—by the time you walk the walk of shame from your last night's date's dorm room, you can safely assume that more than you two know about what happened. Lesson: There are eyes and ears in places you never thought to look.

Try to be smooth about ending relationships with someone on your campus. Also, as hard as you can, try not to date two people who are roommates—at the same time or in sequence—TAs, or professors. Some of each happens each year on almost all campuses, and even if you can pull it off, you can run into serious trouble. Dating professors is especially risky, and in most colleges, you and the professor will both face serious repercussions.

Although dating your dormmates is a bit like dating your siblings—you'll know what we mean after about a month on campus—it does happen from time to time. Not a great idea, for all the obvious reasons you can definitely think of. If you do end up in this situation, avoid offending your other dormmates: Don't make out in the hallway, and try not to isolate yourselves by ignoring them.

Let's Talk About Sex

You know all of this already, of course, but please allow a few brief reminders:

- **Not everyone is doing it.** Yep, you heard us. Many more people than you probably think are waiting until they get married or fall in love, or are waiting just because they feel like waiting. No rule says that because you're in college you're supposed to be having sex. So don't feel pressured and don't drive yourself crazy about it. It's one of the most personal choices you'll ever make, and it's absolutely no one else's business.

- **Be protected.** If you're in college, chances are you do not want to have a baby, so take preventive measures—regardless if you're a guy or a girl, it's your responsibility. Use a condom—if used correctly, they prevent more than 90 percent of pregnancies and also protect you from sexually transmitted diseases (STDs). Most college health centers give them out for free and without embarrassing lectures. Always have one with you and a few in your room. Birth control pills are also a popular method for many women, and are extremely effective, but they don't protect against STDs. If you use any other form of birth control than a condom, you must use a condom to protect against STDs. Period.

"Don't think that it's only sketchy people who have STDs. Anyone who is sexually active is at risk. There is no harm in asking a partner about their history. If they laugh at you, then they're not worth being with anyway."

—Sophomore, Union County College

- **Talk to your partner about birth control and STDs.** Sex is something wonderful and intimate between people who care for each other. But it's not the same as sharing a cozy cup of cocoa on a cold night—it comes with many more risks and potential repercussions. Be confident enough in your partner to talk about things that affect both of your lives. Ask whether he or she has been HIV-tested and tested for other STDs, like hepatitis or gonorrhea. Suggest that both of you get tested before having sex. If you don't feel comfortable enough to talk to your partner about these issues, reconsider your relationship.

- **Emergency contraceptives can be an option.** If you've had unprotected sex or a condom you were using broke, you have less than seventy-two hours to get yourself to the health

Allison's Corner

My friend and her boyfriend were using a condom and it broke. That night they walked to the health center to get emergency contraception. The nurse said that he was the only male she had seen accompany his partner. My friend took the pill but then cried for the next few days because the chemicals were messing with her hormones. It was a frightening experience but she was glad she could get free, confidential help.

center, where they can usually help you. Do not be ashamed. Sure, you may be embarrassed, but the nurses are there to help you and the consequences you're facing are serious enough to warrant being mature. If you're the guy in this scenario, please, go with your partner. This is not an easy time, and your support can be really helpful.

Don't Joke About It

Some pretty awful and scary stuff can happen at college, and you should know how to see it coming and how to protect yourself from sexual assault and date rape. Sexual assault is basically any sexual advance to which you have not consented. Date rape is rape by someone who is not a stranger—a friend, a date, or someone you've met at a party. Women are more often the victims of both and should always be alert, especially when walking alone at night and while at parties.

Guys, don't skip this section—you need to be aware of what can happen to avoid getting into a bad situation yourself and to watch out for your female friends.

Like any dangerous situation, prevention is the key. Go to parties with a buddy who can make sure you're okay. Don't drink excessively if you are in a strange place or without friends. Being drunk or being alone with someone who is extremely drunk greatly increases the risks that something you don't want will happen.

Watch your drink at all times. Date rape drugs can be easily slipped into your drink. Do not let anyone pour it for you behind the bar or let someone else get it for you. Cans of beer are great because when unopened you know there is nothing besides beer

Allison's Corner

I went to a party with a lot of friends and had a glass of punch. The next thing I remember is waking up in my friend's room with no recollection of how I got there. Apparently, I had only one glass of punch, got dizzy and threw up, so they took me home and put me to bed.

I then woke up with the worst hangover ever and threw up again the next morning. Whether something was in my drink or it was simply too strong, it was really disconcerting to black out like that. Luckily, I was in trustworthy hands so I was safe, but I learned my lesson. I now don't drink punch and always watch my drink being poured. Going out with friends secured my safety, and luckily this scary experience didn't turn tragic. This wasn't date rape, but it was the closest to danger I've ever been.

in them. Never leave your glass unattended, and keep your hand over the opening at all times.

Never leave a party with someone you do not wholly trust; if you do, at least tell a friend where you're going. Unfortunately, even a friend can be a date rapist. Be aware of your surroundings and be selective about whom you see alone, especially in very secluded places.

Be forceful when saying no. Do not be coerced by pressure or force. Seek help immediately if you're assaulted. Rape kits can help identify your attacker, and speaking up can save other victims.

If you find yourself in a scary situation, make excuses to leave. Use your cell phone for emergencies. Learning simple self-defense can make you feel safe—there are usually classes on campus.

Sexual assault and date rape are serious issues, and a short section of advice can't really do them justice. Be aware, learn to be safe, and don't let your guard down.

8

The Freshman Fifteen and Other Maladies

Staying in shape and generally healthy at college can be a challenge. You're working and partying a lot, eating at weird times of the day, not getting enough sleep, and living in extremely close proximity to other people. You have to make an effort to take care of yourself because being sick and being at school is no fun at all.

And what about this infamous "Freshman Fifteen?" Sure, some freshman gain a bit of weight during the year, and most college cafeterias make this way too easy. Not everyone gains fifteen pounds, and many of us who gained weight freshman year lost it later as we got used to the funky dynamics of college life. We've included some tips in this chapter for how to stay in shape, but remember, some weight gain is normal as your body continues to grow and develop.

- Skip the Cheese Fries
- Get Your Heart Pumping
- Don't Obsess About Your Weight
- Get Your As, Bs, Cs, and Zs
- Ahh, the Snooze Button!

Skip the Cheese Fries

"A little card to swipe whenever you want to eat is a terrible conspiracy against those who want to maintain a healthy weight. This magical card makes it okay to get a cookie because you're not directly paying for it. It is also your token to the all-you-can-eat buffet. Beware!"

—Sophomore, University of Vermont

Eating at college is usually a social activity, and it's easy to not notice what you're putting in your mouth. Consuming large amounts of alcohol, eating fried cafeteria food, and eating at random times during the day is not great for your gut. Try to remember that and try to eat healthily to stay healthy and maintain a healthy body. You need to feel well on the inside and outside, and what you eat affects both.

"I came to college set on proving the 'freshman fifteen' thing wrong. But I learned that it's hard to stay healthy when every night you're surrounded by pizza, Chinese food, and donuts. My trick? The fridge is always filled with tons of fruit to help resist the late-night pizza order."

—Freshman, Emory University

The basic idea you should try to stick to is trying to eat as healthy as possible as often as possible. There's really no need for strict diets or padlocks on your dorm room fridge. Here are a few practical suggestions for how to accomplish the above:

- **Drink water constantly!** It's weird: There's nothing in it, just clear wet stuff, but water is something we need to consume in large quantities. It keeps you hydrated, washes out things that have no business settling in your body, and can even satisfy hunger—often when you think you're hungry, you're actually thirsty. Buy a large water bottle and keep refilling it throughout the day. Put it next to your computer and take a sip every few minutes. Drink some before going to class and when you come back to your room.

- **Try to eat one healthy meal a day.** If you have pancakes for breakfast and are going out for burgers for dinner, have a salad and soup, or a turkey sandwich, minus a ton of mayo, for lunch.

- **Don't deny yourself all fun food.** It's hard to pass up those cheese fries at lunch, but try to limit them to once a week. If you have to have ice cream, stop at one scoop or try frozen yogurt instead. If you deny yourself what you love, you'll obsess about it constantly and might end up binge eating it later. Instead, have some, but just not in huge quantities or all the time.

- **Don't eat as a procrastination method.** Do something else instead—go for a walk, call a friend, surf the Internet, talk to your roommate, whatever. If you're prone to eating when

Culinary Delights
by David, Junior, Oberlin College

When I came home for winter break, all of the adults had one question for me: "So how's the food there?" "The chef dries out the filet mignon a little, but you can usually trust the foie gras," I wanted to reply. What do they expect? The dining hall is probably the only place where you won't find any difference between your top university and any other college in this country.

The key is to get creative.

Know the salad bar like the back of your hand. Even if the vegetables don't look vine-ripened, here's a hint: If the produce looks old, assume the meat is, too, and it's a lot harder to get food poisoning from veggies. Tossing the salad can be problematic. I recommend taking two bowls, one filled with lettuce and the other with dressing, putting one on top of the other so that they form a sphere, and shaking them to toss the ingredients. Let them stare and drool while you enjoy your perfectly tossed salad.

For the second course, pick the most edible entrée and doctor it up at the salad bar and/or the spice rack. Nine meals out of ten will probably feature spaghetti and tomato sauce (i.e., catsup and ground mystery meat). Try asking for the plain pasta, grabbing a chicken breast from the sandwich/grill section along with cheese and vegetables from the salad bar to finish your pasta primavera. Too fancy? Take a bagel or an English muffin, spread tomato sauce over the top, and add cheese. Throw it in the microwave for a couple minutes and you'll have better pizza than the dining staff will make all year.

There's no accounting for taste, and you may not appreciate my culinary genius, but be sure to experiment for yourself, because you'll waste a lot of money and gain a lot of weight ordering Chinese every night.

you're bored or frustrated, get out of the area where food is readily available.

- **Keep snack food in your room out of sight.** Temptation is often stronger than the strongest of will powers.

- **Remember that alcohol is empty calories.** An average beer has about 100–150 calories. Just keep that in mind.

- **Avoid overeating the five Cs.** Watch out for cookies, cake, chocolate, chips, and candy.

Get Your Heart Pumping

The best way to keep off unwanted pounds and be healthy is to exercise. Not only does exercise build muscle, burn calories, and strengthen your heart, it also fills your mind with all sorts of positive thoughts and helps keep your hands away from junk food. Enough to convince you to try it?

The key about exercising at college is not to get bored. If you get bored, then you're less likely to get enough of it or do it at all. Be creative—there are so many ways to get your body moving and your heart pumping. You can go running, walking, climb the stairs, lift weights, spend twenty-five minutes on the treadmill or the StairMaster, or play a sport. Vary what you do from day to day and week to week and you'll be less likely to lose interest. Varying your exercise also keeps your body on its toes. It doesn't get used to any one kind of activity and you burn more calories that way.

The other thing you have to do is figure out a way to consistently squeeze exercise into your busy schedule. The easiest thing is to say that you have too much to do and can't find time for exercise in your day.

Here are a few ideas of how to approach exercising at college:

- **Get some kind of exercise a few times a week.** It would be nice if you could get the recommended thirty minutes of exercise four times a week, but whoever made the recommendation hasn't lived the crazy life of a college freshman. Don't worry too much about counting minutes—just do something to get your heart pumping a few times a week. After a while, you'll get used to it and will miss it if you don't (a good thing). Go running on the weekends or after a big test to relieve stress, check out the gym a few times, or play an intramural sport.

- **Schedule exercise like a class.** If you find that you need structure to get exercise into your busy life, schedule it like you do your classes. Write it in your planner and treat it as something you have to do.

"If you have a two-hour block of time between your classes on Mondays, Wednesdays, and Fridays, tell yourself that you're going to go to the gym, write it down in your planner, and do it. If you make exercise part of your routine, you won't have to deal with deciding whether or not to go, and deciding to do work or sleep instead—as I did many times—and vowing to go the next day."

—Sophomore, Brown University

- **Take a gym class.** Gym class is a great way to get some exercise into your day as well as add some credits. See what your school offers.

Comic Relief: *Gym Class*
by Jay, Junior, Columbia University

This is a true story about a jump rope and a hapless, uncoordinated freshman trying to fulfill a gym requirement. Let me give you some idea of just how incompetent I am in gym class. I was doing some sort of bizarre stretch when my teacher gave me the following advice: "Breathe." I needed to be reminded to stay alive! "One, two, three, keep that heart pumping blood, four . . ."

I couldn't do sit-ups or push-ups, either. And I couldn't move my feet because they would stick to the floor. Some days, I was amazed I could walk across the aerobics room floor without falling over.

My arch-nemesis in gym class was a black plastic cord an eighth of an inch in diameter and a little less than twice my height. Apparently, the goal was to swing the rope over and under my body, and jump over the rope as it passed. Hopping on one foot. Alternating feet.

It turns out that this is harder than it sounds. I spent the semester whacking my feet, neck, and face with a heavy lump of rope, while I would have preferred to whack my classmates who were able to pick up jumping rope within ten minutes.

By the end of the semester, I was able to jump rope—alternating feet—with the most mediocre of them. Still, my calves thanked me the following semester when I took tai chi. What a relief! Previous gym classes consisted of twenty-five sit-ups, twenty-five push-ups, and forty jumping jacks. But in tai chi class, the teacher says, "Okay, spread your feet shoulder width and try to stay rooted to the ground. But keep your head up. Okay, you're tired. Take a break." The only real challenge was keeping a straight face. That, and doing the tai chi correctly.

- **Work out with a friend.** This can be really great for staying motivated. You'll have someone else to bug you to go and exercise, and someone to chat with as you do. Sometimes we need to be accountable to someone else than just ourselves.

- **Play a sport.** If you're at all interested in sports, it's a great way to get exercise. And you don't have to sign over your life, either—joining an intramural team leaves you much flexibility and free time in your schedule.

Don't Obsess About Your Weight

It's pretty easy to drive yourself crazy about those few extra pounds. You're stressed otherwise—about your classes, adjusting to new places, and new people—and don't really need to deal with this. Magazines with skinny models are all around, and when you turn on the TV, no one seems to look anything like you or your friends. You pinch your waist and your arms and look at your butt in the mirror every ten minutes. You swear off all food above 1,000 calories and spend hours in the gym. The scale becomes your worst enemy, you're anxious all the time, and all you can think about is losing those few pounds.

We know, we've all probably been there some time or another, and often during frosh year. Girls probably obsess about weight lots more than guys, but it's an issue that affects both sexes.

Try as hard as you can to keep your weight in perspective. A few extra pounds aren't really the end of the world, and you can definitely lose them if you want to (check the previous sections). Truly. If not during the year, then during the summer

Allison's Corner

I gained around ten pounds freshman year and was not very happy about it. I tried to keep up with my exercising, but I never found a set schedule and was often at the library too late or couldn't get up early enough to go running. I basically ran out of time to exercise, and eating right was hard when the soft-serve ice cream is free and beer flows on the weekends. I'm learning to adjust to my new body and accept my weight gain as a part of getting older. However, I am working on losing the weight so I can get into a healthy routine. I guess I fell into the trap that most other freshmen do, so now that I've learned my lesson, I can hopefully use some will power and motivation to shed the added ten pounds.

when you're back at home and away from college stress and cafeteria junk food.

Instead of obsessing, take action. Eat healthier. Exercise more often. Snack on carrots instead of chips. Go running when you feel like crying over the few extra pounds. Take a weightlifting class. Do something to solve the problem—it will make you feel in control.

If you really feel like your weight obsession is taking over your life, consider getting some help. It's not embarrassing or silly. Go to the health center and see a nutritionist for some advice. Perhaps consider meeting with a counselor who can help sort out your feelings and get you on the right path of action. Many find it helpful to join a support group, but it can be intense, so think carefully. Whatever you do, don't isolate yourself.

Some of us, mostly guys, get caught up in the opposite of weight loss—weight gain. You're at the gym with some buffer and bigger classmates, and you desperately want to be buffer and bigger. Great. Just don't go overboard, and be careful with any supplements that you take. Take a weightlifting class and talk to a trainer to get some advice.

 ## A Word on Eating Disorders

Eating disorders are a serious problem on college campuses. Anorexia and bulimia affect women more often than men and can truly wreck your life. Each is a pretty complicated disease, often tied in closely to your psyche and overall self-image, and we won't pretend to be able to give advice about dealing with an eating disorder in a few paragraphs.

What we do want to do is alert you to the fact that many college women have eating disorders, and that if you do or you think that you might, or you're obsessing about your weight and it's wrecking your life, you should get counseling and help. There are many hotlines, support groups, and counselors standing by to give you a hand, and you should feel smart and strong for taking it, not weak and stupid. Recognize that an eating disorder is a medical condition, a disease, and just like with other diseases, you need professional help to beat it.

If you suspect that your friend has an eating disorder, judge to see if you can directly confront her or use more subtle hints to direct her toward help. Some people respond better to direct confrontations, but for others it can be a painful blow that won't lead to positive change. Be sensitive and try to help by getting your friend to see a professional counselor or join a support group.

Get Your As, Bs, Cs, and Zs

It's pretty easy to get sick at college: You don't sleep enough, eat unhealthy food, live in extreme proximity to many other people, and are often stressed. This means your immune system is basically calling out to diseases. Getting sick at school is the worst because there is no one to take care of you and no one has the time to sympathize. You can call your mom and cry, but it's your responsibility to care for your physical and mental health.

Take a daily vitamin. It won't ward off all colds and sickness, but it will help.

If you do get sick and get a cold—the most frequent college disease—don't just sit and hope it goes away. It will, but you should help it go away sooner. Drink a ton of water. It will flush out microbes from your body. Drink warm liquids like tea and lots of orange juice for vitamin C. You should also take some vitamin C. Some students swear by Echinacea and zinc when they have a cold. If taken right when you feel the first symptoms coming on, they seem to make the cold milder for some. Oh, and try to get more sleep and pray to the Cold Gods that you'll get better before getting worse.

If you're sick for more than a few days or your symptoms are severe, go to the health center. Don't wait.

Mono (Infectious Mononucleosis) is a serious college campus plague. It's caused by a virus, and its main claim to fame is that it makes you really, really tired. As a virus, it can be spread through bodily fluids—kissing, sharing beer cups, water bottles, etc. Mono usually goes away after a few weeks, but those few weeks can be really exhausting.

If you feel extremely tired for long periods of time, your

throat hurts, and you have a fever, go to the health center. They will tell you to get a ton of rest, take a Tylenol or an Advil, and drink water nonstop. And they will also give you a note for your professors, who should be kind enough to understand that you won't be getting all of your work in on time.

Ahh, the Snooze Button!

"After working out, studying, partying, and hanging out, slumber usually ends up on the bottom of my list. Sleeping in on weekends is the highlight of my week."

—Sophomore, West Chester University

Try to get at least six hours of sleep on most nights. It will not always be possible, like when it's midnight and you haven't started a paper due the next morning, or when you stayed late at a party and have to get up early for your intramural baseball game. Excuses for not getting enough sleep in college are endless, and many are valid. But do yourself a favor and try to squeeze in time for sleep.

Strategic power naps are key. Since college is not like high school and your day is made up of chunks of activities rather than one block, you can find a few minutes to take a nap. Ten, twenty, or thirty minutes in the afternoon can really do wonders for your energy level. Close the blinds, put on some mellow music, and ask your roommate not to talk on the phone. Ah . . . college naps are wonderful moments of rest and peace you'll quickly learn to appreciate.

9

Managing Life Stuff

If sharing a tiny room with a new person, studying, extracurriculars, partying, and staying healthy weren't enough, you've got to take care of your finances, your safety, and the safety of your valuables. Phew!

All it takes is a bit of organization and planning, and managing these responsibilities will become second nature soon enough. Here are a few things to keep in mind.

- Money Management 101
- Get a Job You Can Handle
- Save Your Moola
- Stay Safe
- Take Care of Your Stuff

Money Management 101

Make Friends with Budgets

Whether you're paying your own bills or your parents are, it's important to keep track of your expenses. It's extremely easy to find things on which you want to spend money, and you need to know if you can afford to plunk down the cash. If you're like the majority of college students, you're already in debt through your loans. The last thing you need is credit card debt.

Create a simple budget for yourself. First, write down your "must pay" expenses—tuition, rent, food, books, school supplies, phone, and travel expenses. Try to estimate carefully what you'll need to pay for these expenses during the year, and then break it down by the month. Then add a few extra expenses like entertainment and clothing—things that you'll want to spend money on but technically could go without.

Now calculate how much money you'll have each month to cover your expenses. You might have a job during the year, or might have saved up during the summer and plan to spend the money during the year. Your parents might be paying for some or all of your tuition, or you might have gotten some loans and scholarships or have some savings that you want to use for college. If your parents are paying for some of your expenses, make sure that you're very clear about exactly which expenses they'll cover. For example, your parents might be paying for books at your college bookstore but not for lattes you get there with friends. Avoid conflict by knowing this up front.

Look at your income and your expenses—hopefully, they're

pretty close. But if you find that your expenses are greater than your resources, go through the list and see where you can cut it down.

On the next page is a simple template that you can use to go through this little exercise—feel free to adapt it to your needs.

Another suggestion we have is to keep a log of your monthly expenses. You can write them down in a notebook or you can use Microsoft Excel (or a similar spreadsheet program) to track what you're spending each month. It's no fun being a penny pincher, but the reality is that most college students live on a budget. Keeping track of your spending will let you see where the money is going, and where you might need to tone it down a bit if you're spending too much.

Bank like a Pro

Find a bank near your school and open an account. You'll be able to withdraw money locally without incurring ATM fees. Withdraw only as much as you realistically need for a week. Carrying a lot of cash on you or keeping it in your room can be dangerous because it's easily lost or stolen. It can also tempt you to spend more than you should.

Be Careful with Credit Cards

It's a good idea to have a credit card for larger expenses. If it's stolen, you're only responsible for about fifty bucks. But before you sign up for a credit card, make sure to learn about its features and get the best one. There will be credit card companies on campus trying to lure you in with offers of free T-shirts and pens, but don't get a card unless you know that it's got what you need.

There are three major types of cards that all get called credit cards:

- **Credit card.** A card that lets you make purchases and then allows you to either pay the entire amount of what you've spent in a given month or just a portion of that amount, with the rest to be paid later with interest.

- **Charge card.** A card that lets you make purchases like a credit card, but that requires that you pay the entire bill in full at the end of the month. In other words, you can't shift your balance and pay some now and some later.

- **Debit card (or Check card).** A card that's linked to your bank account and that allows you to make purchases without using cash. Every time you make a purchase, the amount of purchase is deducted from your bank account, and you can't charge more on the card than you have in your account. Debit cards are accepted wherever you see the logo featured on the card—if it's a MasterCard, then you can use it wherever you see the MasterCard logo.

On the next page we've included a list of the main credit card features that you need to consider.

If at all possible, try to avoid running a balance on your credit card. Listen to all those horror stories about students getting deep into credit card debt and believe that they can happen to you. Try to pay off the bill in full each month and record your credit card expenses in your monthly budget.

Monthly Budget Template

In most cases, you'll pay tuition and room and board once every semester, so we won't include these expenses in the monthly budget. You should know, from your annual budget, how much money you have to save during the year and each month to pay for your share of tuition and room and board, so we've included that as an expense in the monthly budget—you should think of it that way and try to put that amount of money in the bank each month.

Expenses		Resources	
Savings contribution		Job/Work-Study	
Books/School supplies		Savings Account	
Meals (if not already paid in meal plan)		Parents	
Take-out/Going out		Other	
Car expenses			
Other travel expenses			
Phone/Internet			
Clothes, CDs, Etc.			
Total		Total	

Take Care of Financial Aid

If you're on financial aid, remember that you have to file new forms, like the Free Application for Student Aid (FAFSA), every year. Make an appointment with a financial aid counselor and

Credit Card Features

Annual Percentage Rate (APR)	This is the interest rate that will be charged to any balance that you revolve on your card—i.e., if you don't pay your monthly balance in full, a percentage will be added to the revolving balance when your bill comes the next month, and so on.	You want your APR to be as low as possible. Be especially careful because often credit card companies will give you a low APR for the first several months, and then hike it after that.
Annual fee	An annual membership fee.	You can definitely get a credit card in college without a membership fee.
Grace period	The number of days you have after the end of one payment period to pay your balance in full and avoid interest charges on new purchases that you made.	Twenty-five days is standard, and you shouldn't get a card that's less than that.
Late payment fee	Amount you'll get charged, on top of any interest charges, if your payment is late.	Usually around $20–$25.
Incentives	Most cards come with incentives. For each dollar you spend you might get frequent flyer miles, free phone minutes, or just dollars that you can spend on whatever you want.	You can usually get a bonus for getting a card for the first time—such as 10,000 frequent flyer miles.

know what you're required to do and by when. Also, just because you're in college doesn't mean that you can't apply for scholarships—many are available, and every little bit helps. You can easily search for scholarships on websites like www.FastWeb.com.

Get a Job You Can Handle

Going to college is a full-time job and then some. Before you get a part-time job during the year, think about whether you really need the money and how it will impact your ability to study, get good grades, socialize, and get the most out of your college experience. If you don't have to work during school to pay bills, you have the ability to really focus on your college studies and experiences, and that's a huge benefit. Consider working during the summer instead of during the year.

 Allison's Corner

I decided I wasn't going to work first semester so that I could get adjusted to school and have time to explore other activities. This worked out well for me because I earned enough money in the summer to support that decision. I did take on temporary jobs such as doing interviews for the public policy center and being a participant in cognitive science experiments on campus. I'd earn quick cash and could schedule when I wanted to work.

If you do have to work during college, look for a job with flexible hours and a location on or close to campus. If you can find a job that pays you to do something you like—tutoring, for example—go for it. You might also be able to get paid for helping a professor with research, which can be a great way to get to know a certain academic discipline in more depth.

If you're on financial aid and can get work-study jobs, you're in luck. Many are easy and allow you to study while you work, and they're on campus, saving you travel time. Go to the financial aid office as soon as you get to campus and check job listings—the best (read: easiest) ones go quickly.

"Desk jobs are the greatest because the school really helps you out by paying you to do minimal work. Although shelving things makes you feel like you're wasting your time, it's a great way to meet other students and bond over your labor."

—Sophomore, Vassar College

Save Your Moola

There are so many ways to save money while in college and still live in style. Be creative, be frugal, and you'll be able to find things for less that you still like.

Here are just a few ideas:

- **Buy used textbooks and books.** College books are extremely expensive, and getting them used can save you a bundle, sometimes more than half of the retail price. Look for used books in your college store and also online—there are many

websites that sell (and buy) used books, such as www.
bigwords.com.

- **Sell your own books at the end of each year.** There are some
that you'll want to keep—particularly if you plan to major
in that field—and some that you'll never read again. Make
sure that you don't ruin books with highlighting and writing too much in the margins, and know your college bookstore's rules about selling used books.

- **Shop at thrift or second-hand stores.** Besides funky clothing,
these stores are great sources for cheap dishes, furniture
pieces, and books.

- **Learn to love Ikea.** No other store we know of has such fun,
functional, and *cheap* furniture and household supplies like
carpets and curtains. Find one in your area and consider
renting a van with a few friends—it's well worth it.

 Allison's Corner

I try very hard to save money and make the most of what I
have. My parents are nice enough to pay for tuition and housing, but I pay for all outside expenses myself. To save money,
I rarely go out to eat. I go shopping at the Salvation Army and
am a fan of bookstore sales and buying used books from other
students.

Stay Safe

"In the rural fields of Ohio, the only things we have to worry about are the cows!"

—Sophomore, Wooster College

Urban campuses have higher crime rates, so if you're in a city, get to know your neighborhood and be aware of boundaries that are safe for you. Don't feel the adventurous need to explore shady areas. For any campus, find out what safety services your school offers. Whether it's a campus shuttle, an escort service, a safe walk home, or those blue-light emergency phones, be familiar with your options.

Walking alone at night can be dangerous, especially for women. Walk with someone else and in well-lit areas. Always be alert to your surroundings and remember that drugs and alcohol make your mind less alert to potential dangers.

If you have a cell phone, carry it with you and make sure the battery is charged. Consider putting a whistle and pepper spray on your key chain. Your voice is an important defense mechanism—if you feel unsafe or are assaulted, scream "Help!" There's always a chance that someone will hear you and come to the rescue.

Take Care of Your Stuff

Getting things stolen out of your room, backpack, or locker sucks, but it does happen. Although you don't want to go around locking up everything you own, getting and using a lock for your bike, laptop, and gym locker is a good idea.

Don't leave expensive or valuable things all around your dorm room, and consider leaving some at home. Lock the door when you're not in, and if you're on the first floor, make sure to close and lock your windows as well.

10

It's Summer Time!

It might not seem possible when you get to campus, but your freshman year will fly by faster than you probably expect. Before you know it, it will be time to pack up and head back home. And while it's definitely tempting to just hop into your or your parents' car and leave all that freshman-year stress behind, you'll thank yourself later if you take care of some last-minute details before you leave.

Here are some things to consider as you get ready to take off.

- Take Care of End-of-Year Logistics
- Will Work for Summer
- Should I Transfer?

Take Care of End-of-Year Logistics

It's pretty exciting to finish your finals and be free for the whole summer of relaxation and fun. But before you get too caught up in the anticipation, make sure you've nailed down a few logistics.

- **Storage.** If you need to store your things for next year, look for storage near your campus. Some schools will have their own storage facilities and some may have a service to help you transport your stuff. Check out your options, and make sure to carefully estimate how much room you'll need.

- **Summer address.** Make sure your school has your correct summer address. You never know what might come up, and you should make it easy for them to reach you.

- **Housing.** You've probably figured out your housing for next year a few months before the end of second semester. If you're rooming with other people or sharing a house, exchange phone numbers or email addresses so that you can coordinate who brings what next year.

- **Books.** Sell your used books before you leave so that you don't have to drag them back and forth.

Will Work for Summer

Having a summer job will get you extra cash, experience, and hopefully something interesting to put on your résumé.

If you're considering an internship, make sure you begin to look and fill out applications a few months before the end of the year. Go to your school's career center and look through internship opportunities—usually there are pretty good campus resources to guide your search. Also check out Internet internship job boards and listings like www.internships.com and www. monstertrak.com.

Another great way to find an internship—and any other job— is by word of mouth. Tell your parents, your professors, and your friends about what you're looking for and ask them to pass it on to anyone they know. A third cousin of your roommate's father's niece might own a great company you want to intern with. You never know.

Temp agencies in your hometown—or wherever you plan to be for the summer—can be a pretty good source of office jobs. Usually these aren't much fun, but you can typically make from $12/hr to $20/hr. Check out what's available in your area.

While it's great to have a summer job that looks amazing on your résumé, you don't have to do it just yet. Find something that's fun, that gives you some extra cash, and try to leave a few weeks just to relax. If you thought frosh year was tough, just wait for the next one.

Should I Transfer?

"Don't think about transferring in the first or the last two weeks of the first semester. The first two weeks, you're not used to school and you haven't seen all it has to offer—you might be overly excited or slightly scared. In the last two weeks, you're worn out from finals and sick of your friends—ready to go home. If you're unhappy mid-semester or second semester when things are stable, then maybe you should consider transferring."

—Sophomore, Claremont McKenna College

During freshman year, everyone has a bad day, a bad week, and sometimes a bad month. This doesn't always mean you should pack up and go. If you're unhappy, you first have to figure out why. Is it your dull classes? Your obnoxious roommate? The pressure of freshman year in general? The rainy weather?

Really think hard and figure out whether your sources of unhappiness can be fixed—e.g., next year you don't have to live with the same roommate and can take smaller classes with more dynamic profs—or not. Transferring is a tough process, and you want to do it only if it's going to benefit you.

Talk to your parents, friends, and professors about your thoughts on transferring. People who know you well often have some great insights. Talk to a few academic advisors and deans as well—they've worked with many students and can help you sort out your feelings and tell you more about the transferring process.

"My thoughts about transferring came perhaps because I was impatient. I didn't realize that the people around me were as cool as those who I had shared my life with until college. But I changed my mind because I gradually got to know the best sides of my new friends."

—Sophomore, New York University

If you do decide to transfer, be prepared to start the college application process from scratch. Hopefully this time you'll have a better idea of what you're looking for. Do your research! Don't exclusively rely on your friends' info about schools, even if they go to the one you're considering. If you can, visit schools you're thinking about. Talk to students, professors, and advisors. Look at your list of reasons for wanting to transfer and see if what you're missing at your school can be found at the new one.

Even if you've made up your mind to transfer and can't wait to leave, maintain a decent GPA so you'll have a respectable transcript. Find out all application requirements for your new school(s) and stick to them.

Transferring schools is not the end of the world. You have not failed. You have not wasted a year, but instead have tested yourself and found out what doesn't work for you. And that's pretty important. Try not to get down about transferring, and look at it as another opportunity to start fresh.

11

The Daily Grind

Here are a few general ideas to keep in mind as you successfully navigate through your freshman-year maze.

Embrace Your Freedom to Make Choices

"The first step to getting the things you want out of life is this: Decide what you want."

—Ben Stein

Freshman year you'll have more freedom to make choices and decisions than probably ever before. Recognize that your choices affect your life and embrace the chance to make them. It can be scary at times, but it's extremely rewarding to feel like you're standing on your own two feet.

Know also that while you're the final judge of what's right for you, you don't have to make decisions in isolation. Seek advice from people you trust, take it with a grain of salt, and your decisions will be that much more informed.

Appreciate Differences

"The highest result of education is tolerance."

—Helen Keller

College exposes you to things you've never heard of before. You'll meet people whose culture may be contradictory to your values or who have ideologies you don't understand.

Learning to appreciate other cultures instead of judging them can spark different interests and make you a well-rounded, better educated human being. Diversity is important, and making friends whose backgrounds are different than yours can truly be enlightening. Don't be a victim of ignorance. Learning to coexist with difference truly is the highest form of education. Enjoy your uniqueness and celebrate others'.

Do Everything with Passion

"Education is not the filling of a pail, but the lighting of a fire."

—W. B. Yeats

If you do what you love, you'll succeed, no question—in college and in life. Search out what you're passionate about and go after it with energy. Many people will have opinions about what you should do, and you should listen to trusted advice.

But only you know what you want to do.

Don't Be Afraid to Make Mistakes

"To get back one's youth, one has to repeat one's follies."

—Oscar Wilde

Being young and being a freshman gives you a license to make mistakes. Take it. The older we get, the higher the stakes, and the more we have to worry about the consequences of doing the wrong thing.

Try new things, test yourself, mess up, and try again. It might not seem so rewarding in the short run, but you'll be able to look back and at least know that you didn't sit safely on the sidelines.

Helpful Resources

Here are some additional resources you might want to consider as you face your first year at college.

Books

What Smart Students Know, by Adam Robinson. Crown Publishing, 1993.

Major in Success: Make College Easier, Fire Up Your Dreams, and Get a Very Cool Job, by Patrick Combs. Ten Speed Press, 4th edition, 2003.

What Every College Student Should Know: How to Find the Best Teachers and Learn the Most from Them, by Ernie Lepore and Sarah-Jane Leslie. Rutgers University Press, 2002.

Making the Most of College: Students Speak Their Minds, by Richard J. Light. Harvard University Press, 2001.

Been There, Should've Done That II: More Tips for Making the Most of College, by Suzette Tyler. Front Porch Press, 2nd edition, 2001.

Ruminations on College Life, by Aaron Karo. Fireside, 2002.

Roget's Thesaurus, the *American Heritage Dictionary*, and the *MLA Handbook*.

Websites

Work and research

www.questia.com   www.essayedge.com

Life as a freshman

www.collegefreshmen.net   www.campusblues.com
www.collegeview.com

Jobs

www.internships.com   www.snagajob.com
www.monstertrak.com   www.quintcareers.com

Moola

www.fool.com   www.fastweb.com
www.finaid.org

Savin' moola

www.bigwords.com   www.campusbooks.com
www.ecampus.com

Fun

www.dailyjolt.com   www.collegeclub.com

The Final Word

Four years is not a huge amount of time. But college, and fresh-man year in particular, is a very intense period, so your life could dramatically change in any single moment. Being introduced to a new idea or a new person has unpredictable potential to alter your future.

Freshman year is never quite what you expect. You may have dreamy ideas about partying until dawn every night or feel terri-fied by the massive piles of books you'll have to read. Whatever your initial idea of college is, chances are that you'll be chal-lenged and surprised, both in and outside of class. And that's perhaps one of the greatest things about it—its ability to shake loose our preconceptions about college and ourselves, and to in-troduce us to a whole new world.

There's no one way to do freshman year right. But there is a way to do it right for you, and hopefully we've given you some ideas for how to do that throughout this book. Don't get frustrated with making mistakes, have fun, and embrace the many opportunities available to you. You can do whatever you like now, so make it something that makes you happy.

And hey, next year you can look at the incoming frosh and sigh in relief—you don't have to do *that* again.

To learn more about Students Helping Students® books, read samples and student-written articles, share your own experiences with other students, suggest a topic, or ask questions, visit us at www.StudentsHelpingStudents.com!

We're always looking for fresh minds and new ideas!

Index

Deans, 27
  help of, 74
Debit Card, 126
Decorating
  in dorm room, 31
Deliverance, 23
Dershowitz, Alan, 90
Dictionary, 7
Differences
  appreciation of, 140
  in college, 140
  in freshman year, 1–2
  meeting people with, 19–20
Dorm Room
  cleanliness of, 37
  decorating in, 31, 35–36
  items for, 30
  moving out of, 43
  multiple roommates, 42–43
  odors in, 37
  privacy in, 38
  singles, 42
  socializing with, 32
  space management in, 35
  visitors in, 40
Dorms
  meeting people in, 40
  noise in, 40
  options in, 42
  resources in, 40
  single varieties of, 42
  socializing in, 40
Drinking. *See also* Alcohol Abuse;
    Alcohol Poisoning; Date Rape;
    Drugs; Hangover
  driving and, 92
  drugs and, 98
  excess of, 92–93, 94, 95, 97
  hangover from, 94
  moderation in, 91
  underage, 93–94
Drinks
  date rape prevention with, 109–10
Drugs, 96–97
  dangers of, 98

Earplugs, 40
Eating
  in college, 112–13
  healthy tips for, 113, 115
  unhealthy college foods and, 112
Eating Disorders, 120
  weight and, 120
Ecstasy, 98
Emergency Contraceptives, 107–8
  examples of, 108
End of year
  logistics of, 135
Escape Pod, 39–40
Exams
  academics in, 66–67
  difficulty of, 67
  studying for, 59–60, 66
  tips for, 66–67
Excess
  of drinking, 92–93, 97
  of extracurricular activities,
    86–87
  of studying, 75
Exercise
  fitness with, 111
  importance of, 115–16
  jumping rope for, 117
  sports for, 118
  tips for, 116, 118
  varieties of, 115
Extensions, 66
Extracurricular activities, 78
  examples of, 81
  excess of, 86–87
  off-campus varieties of, 79
  personal enjoyment of, 84
  taking chances with, 81
  time consumption with, 85
  time management with, 85

FAFSA. *See* Free Application for
    Student Aid
Felicity, 21
Finances, 123, 130–31
Financial Aid, 127–28

Students Helping Students®
Get the whole series of guides written *for* students *by* students.

Available April 2005

NAVIGATING YOUR
FRESHMAN YEAR

0-7352-0392-X

GETTING THROUGH
COLLEGE WITHOUT
GOING BROKE

0-7352-0393-8

HAVE NO
CAREER FEAR

0-7352-0394-6

Available August 2005

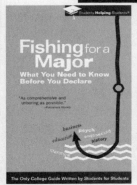

FISHING FOR A
MAJOR

0-7352-0395-4

TACKLING THE
COLLEGE PAPER

0-7352-0397-0

CHOOSE THE RIGHT
COLLEGE AND GET
ACCEPTED

0-7352-0396-2